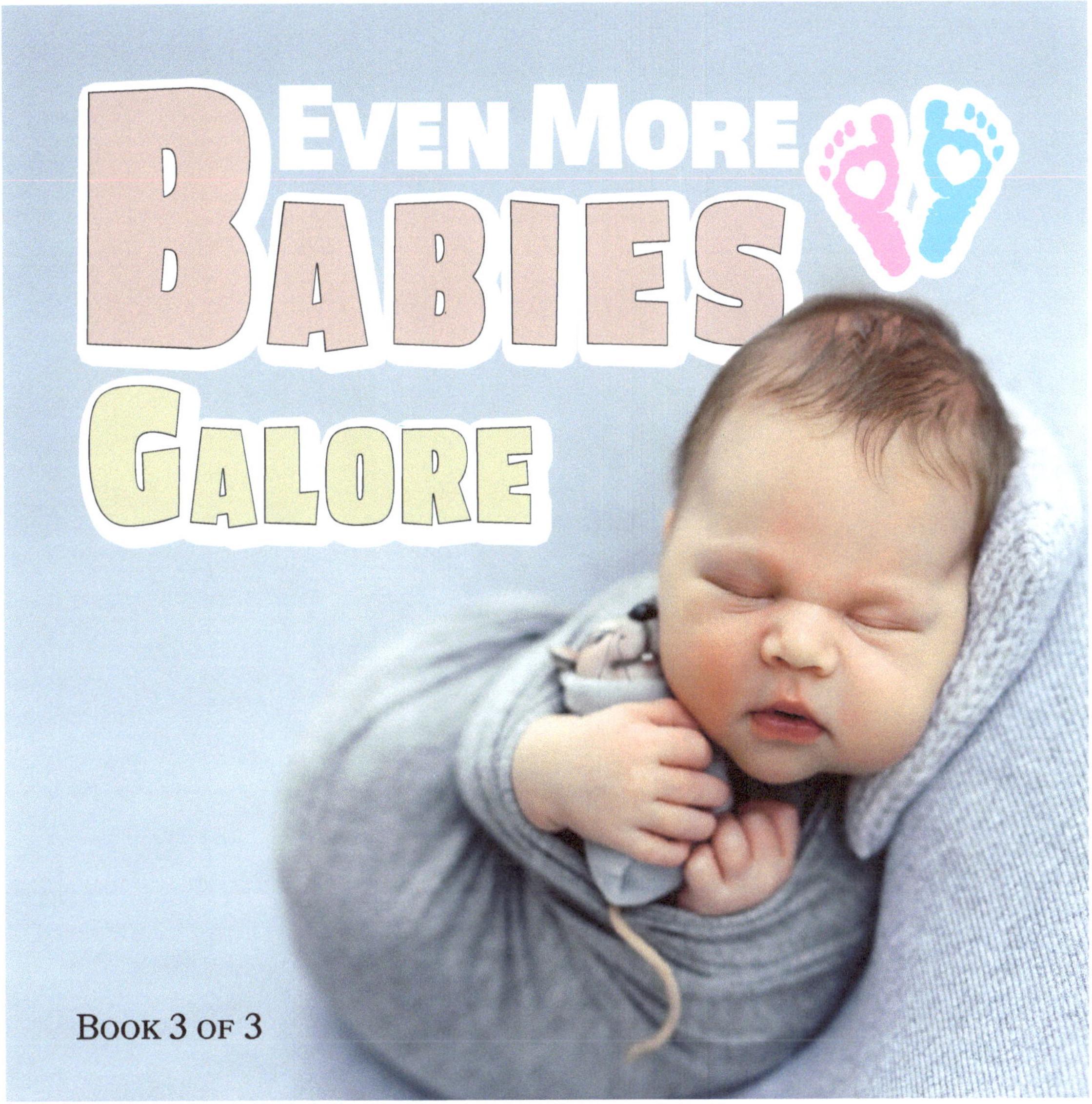

ISBN: 978-1-989842-12-6

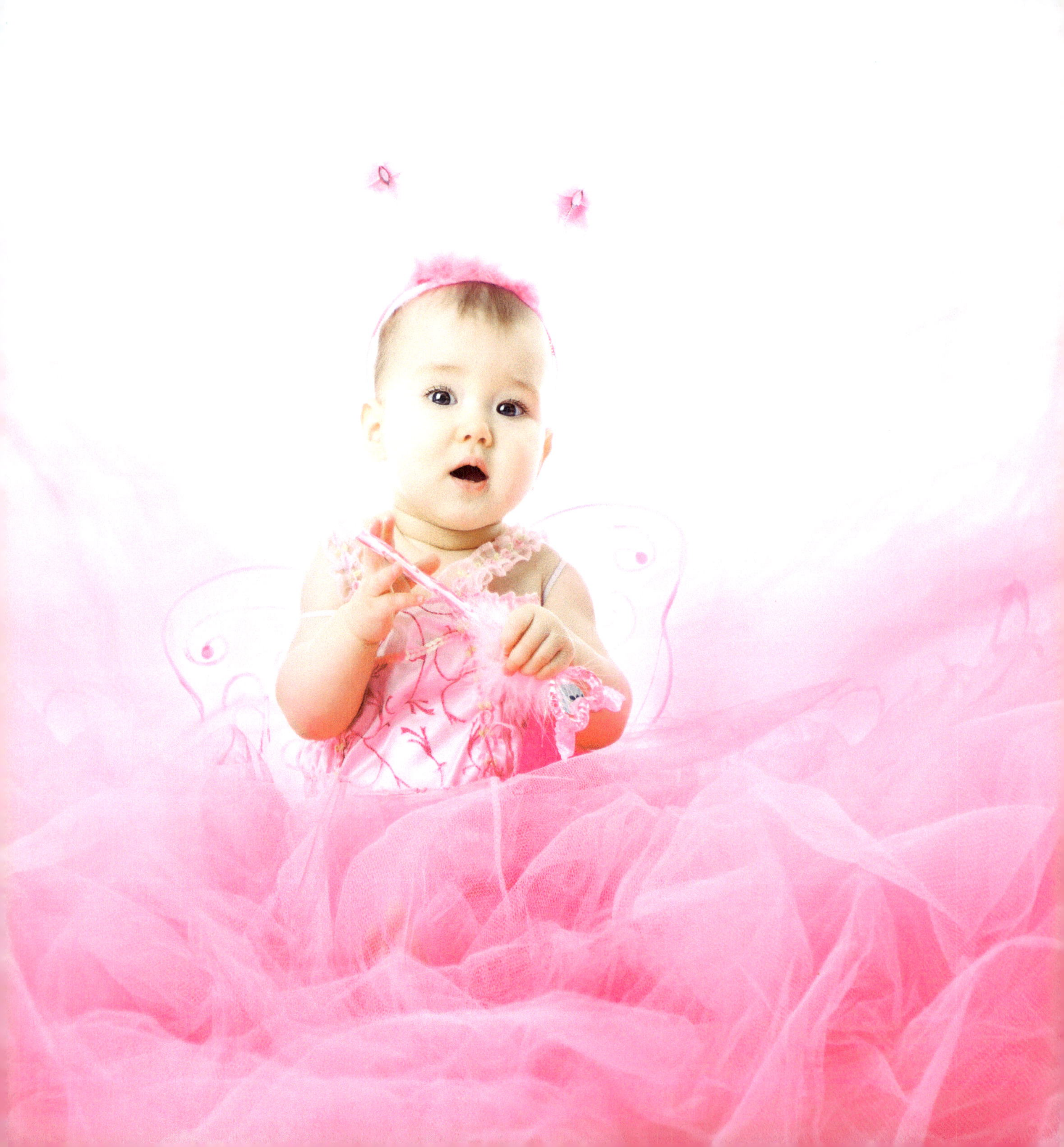

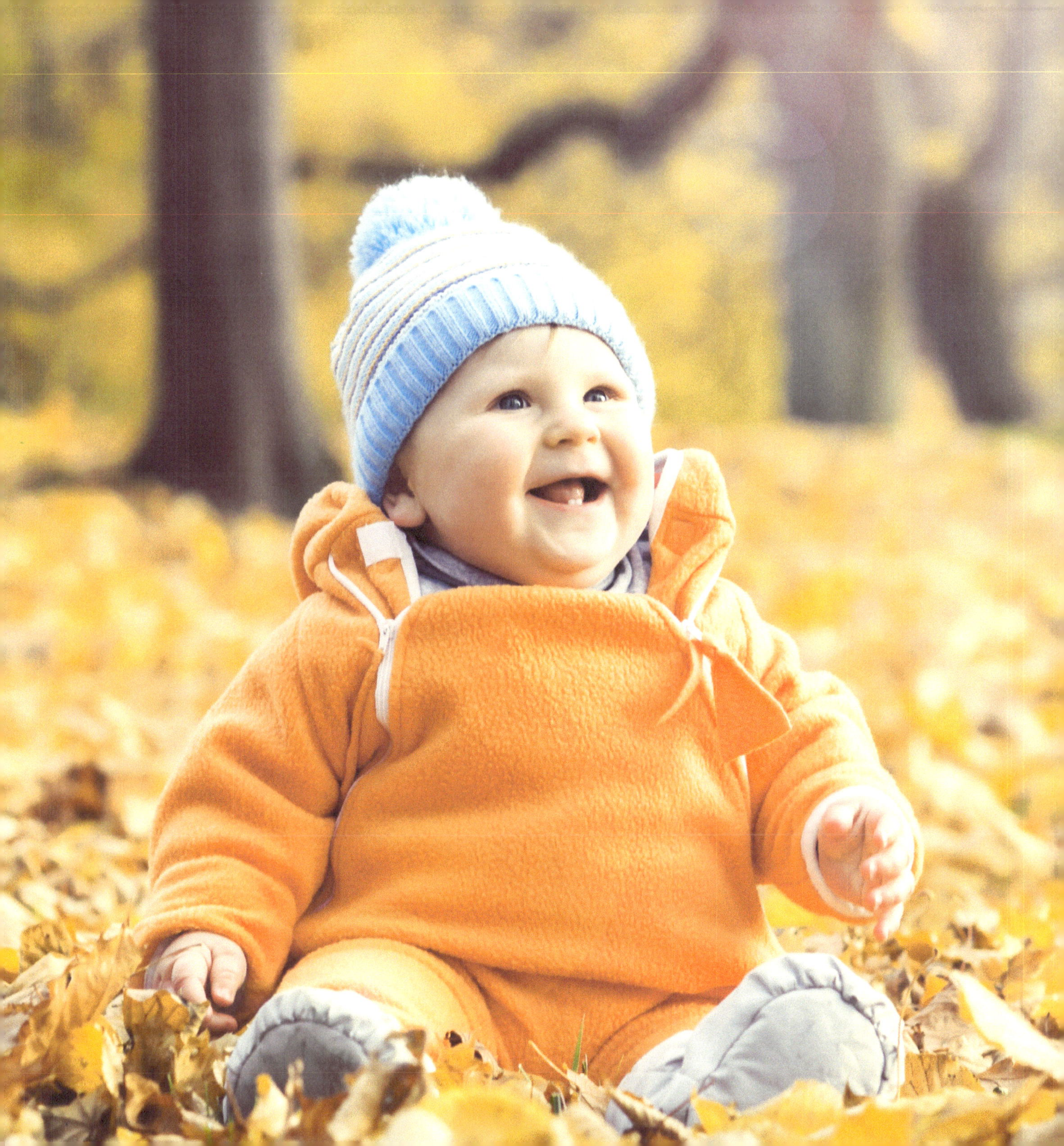

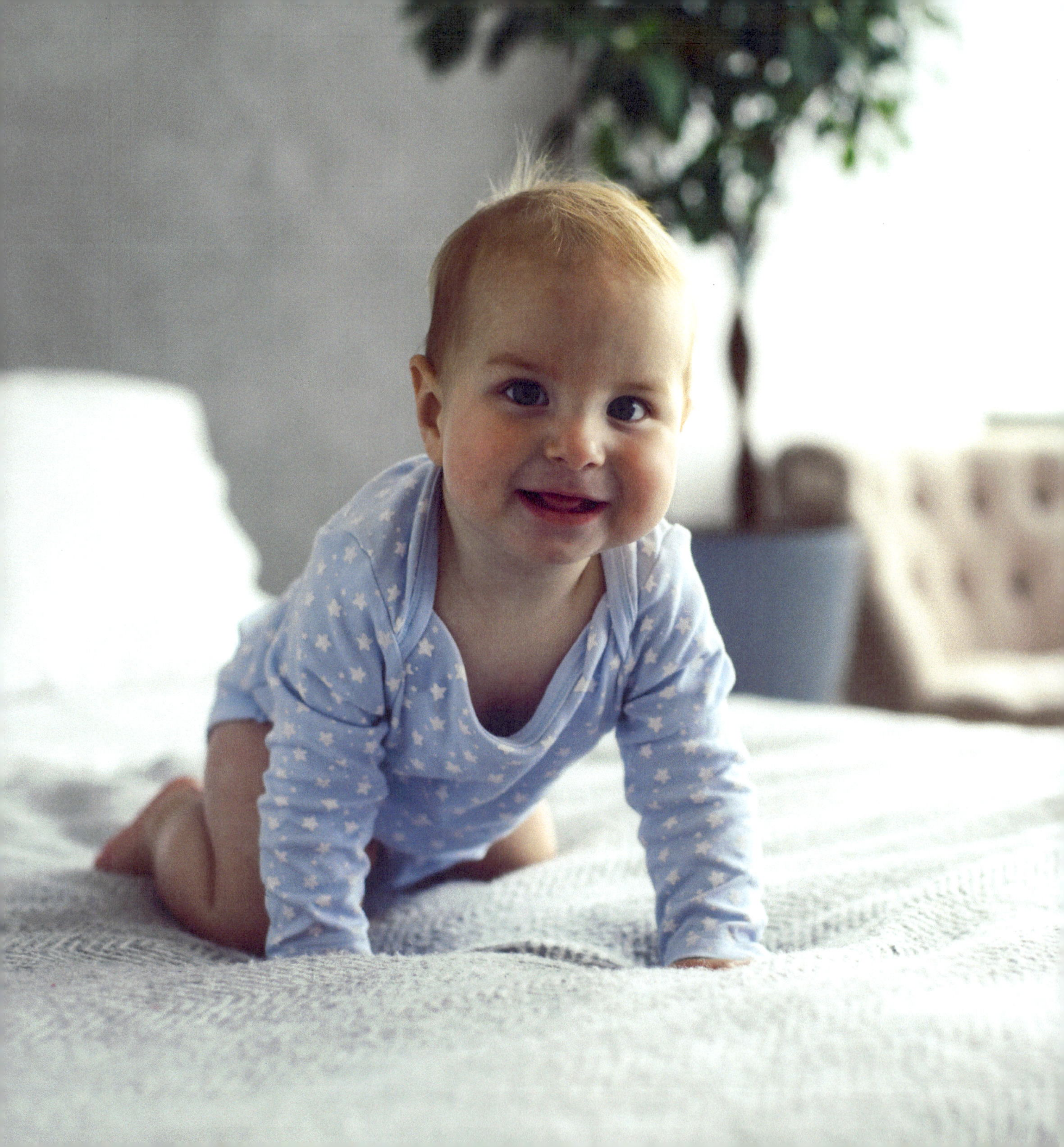

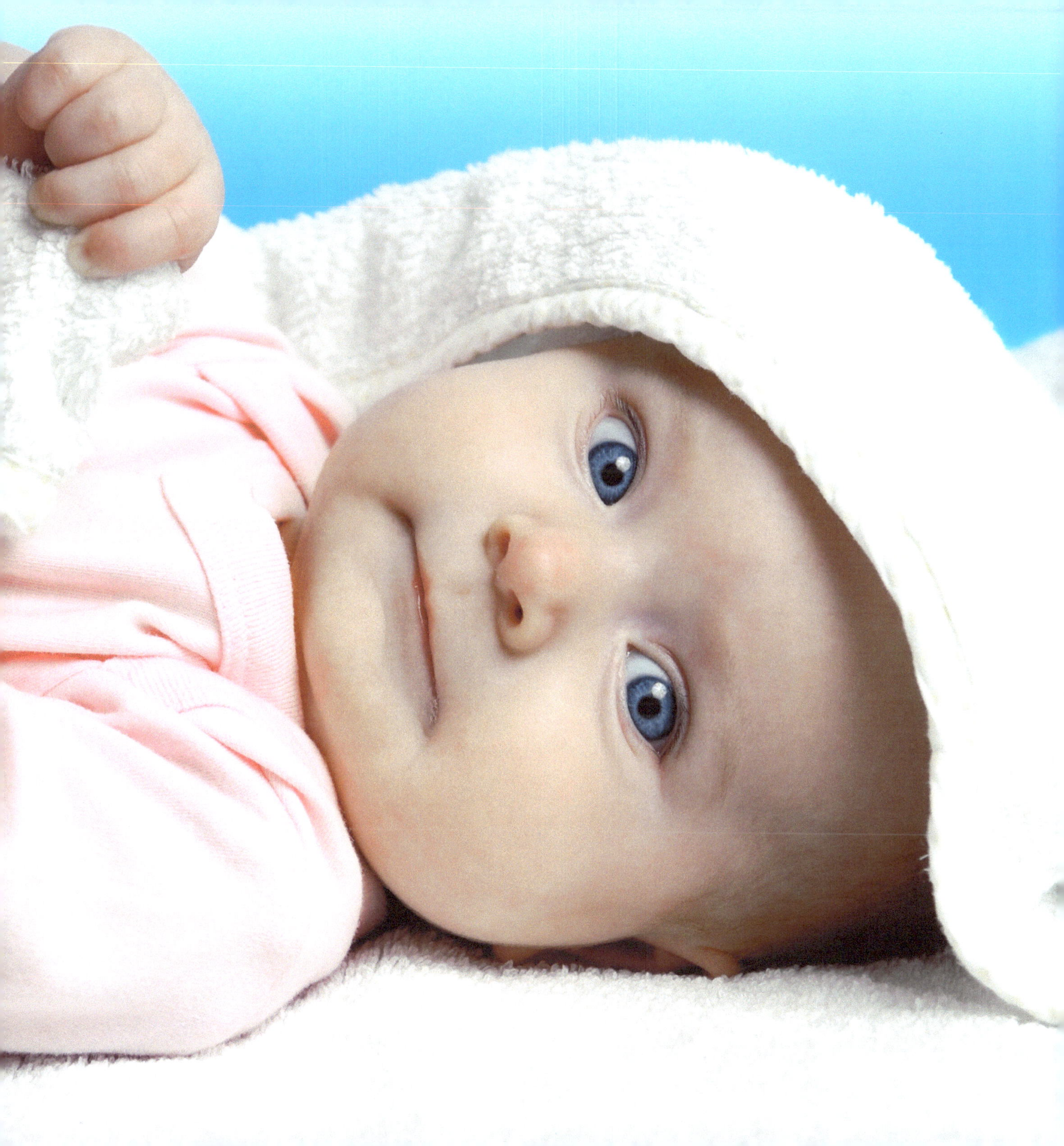

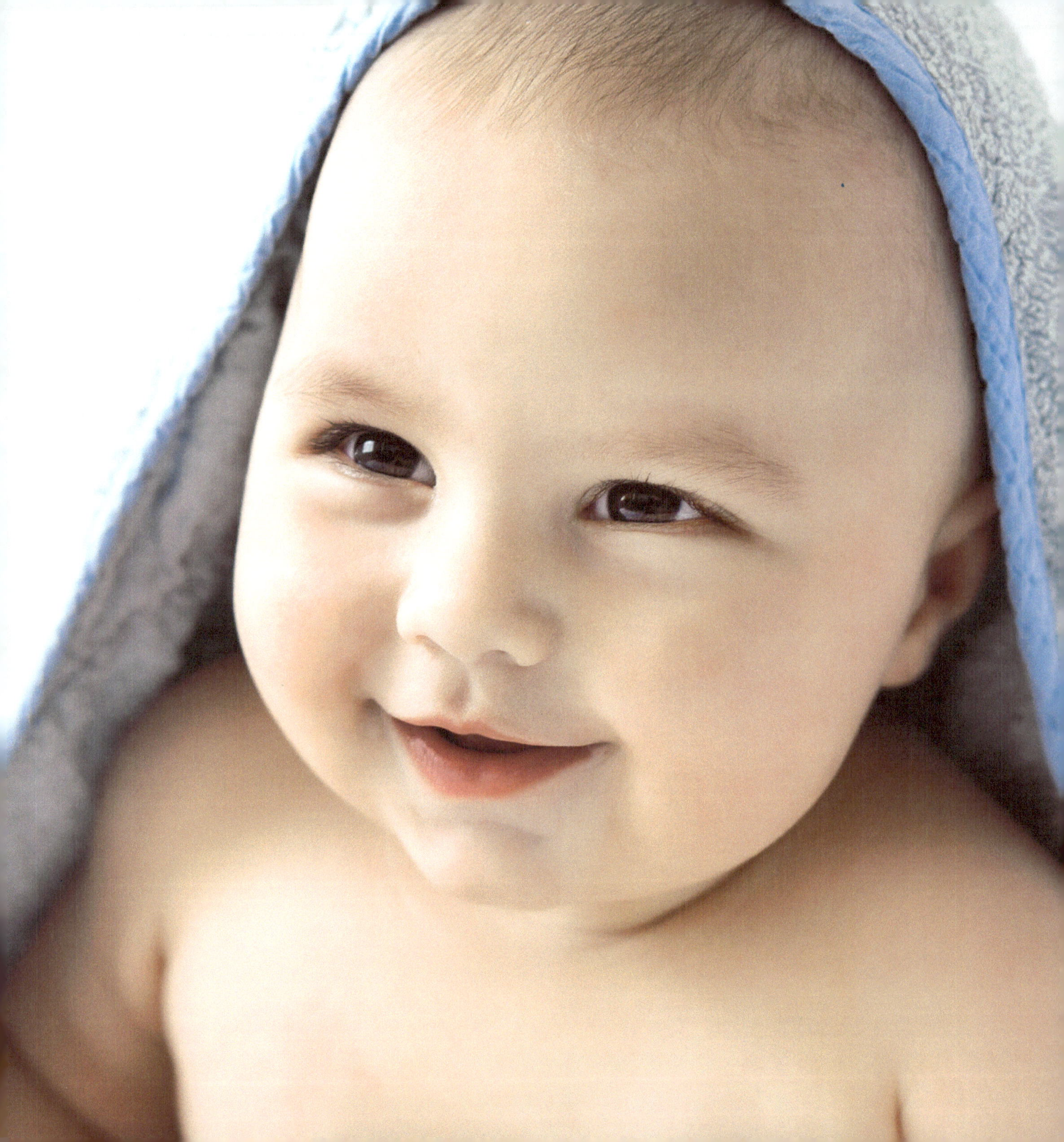

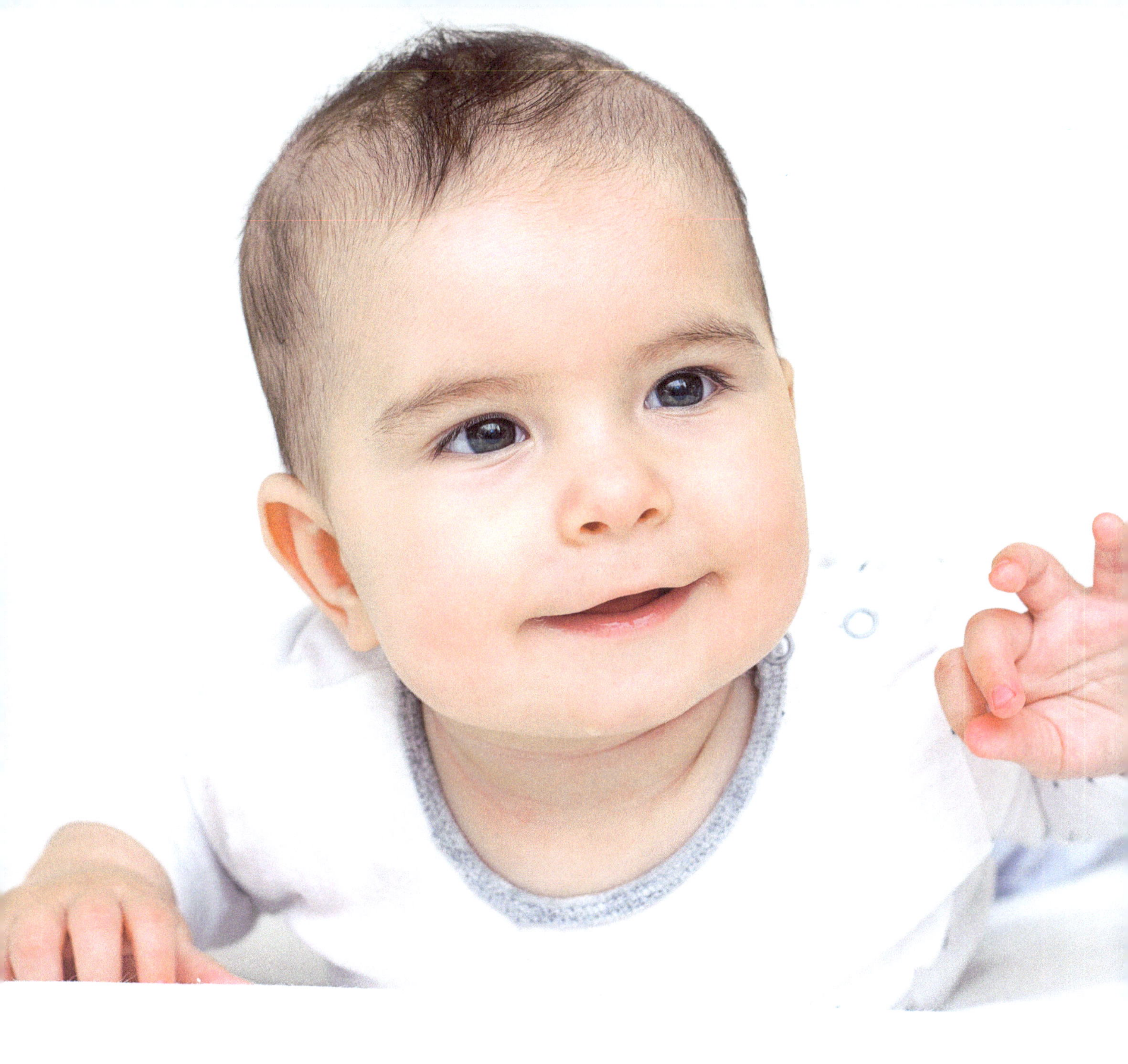

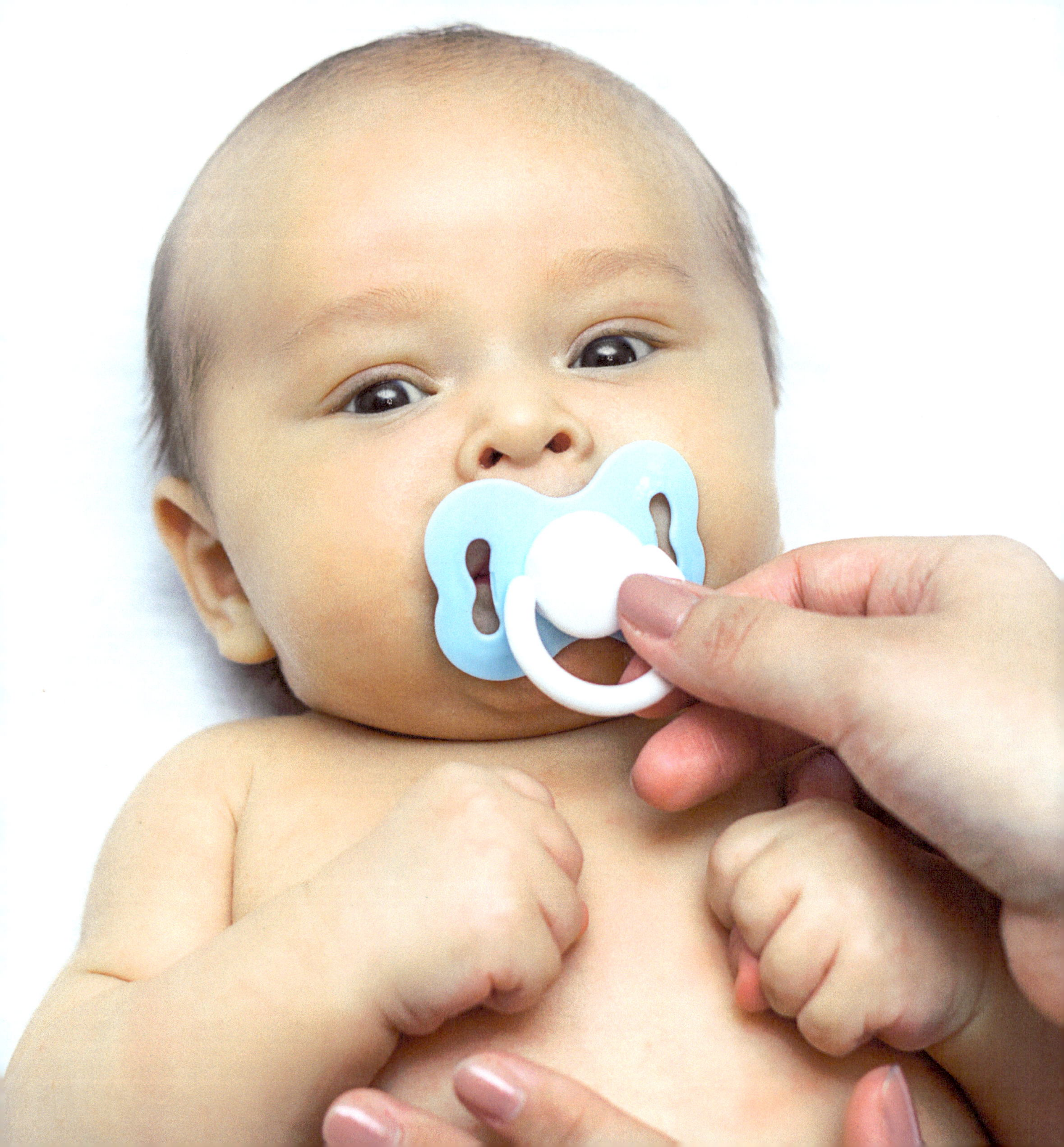

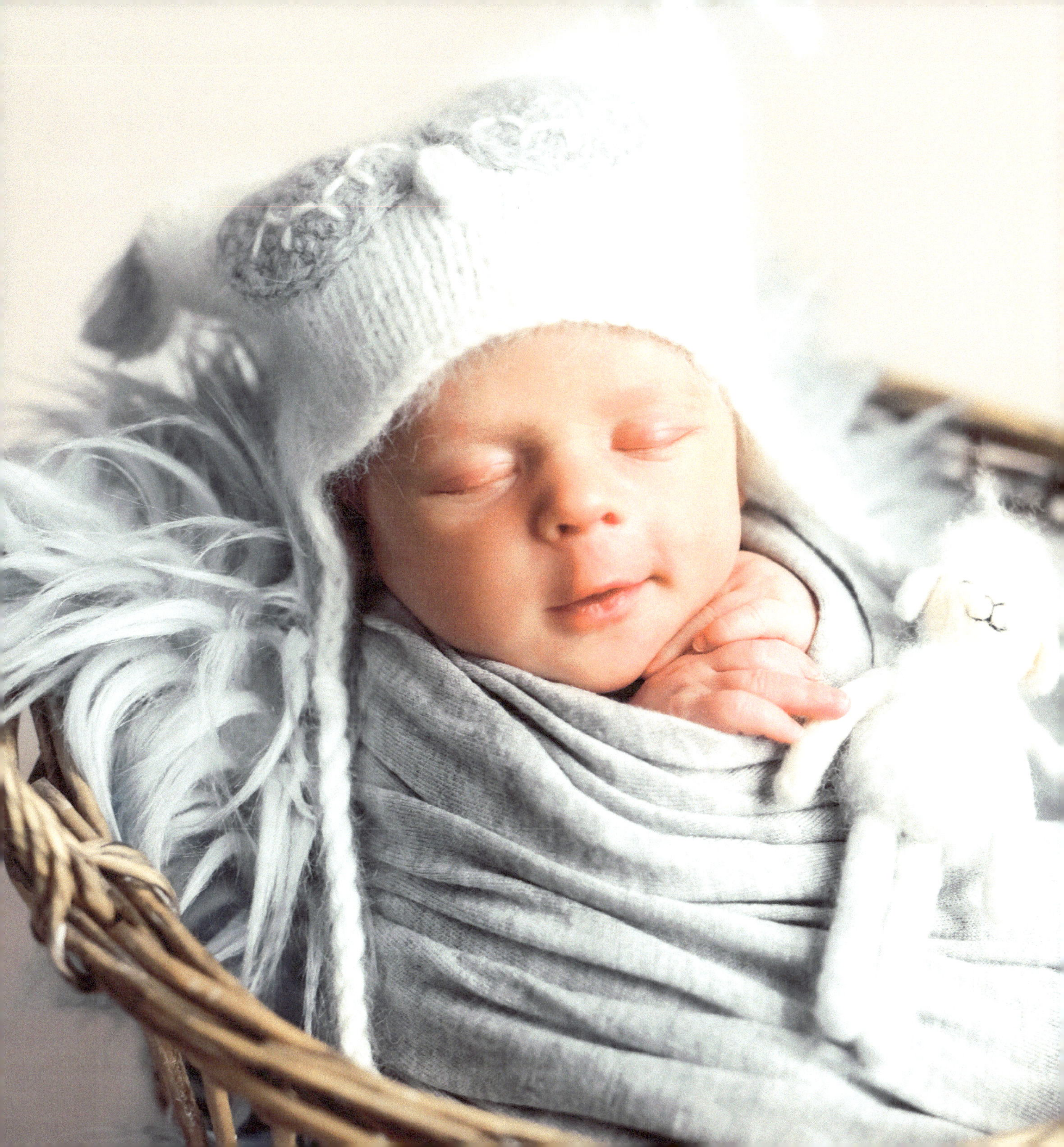

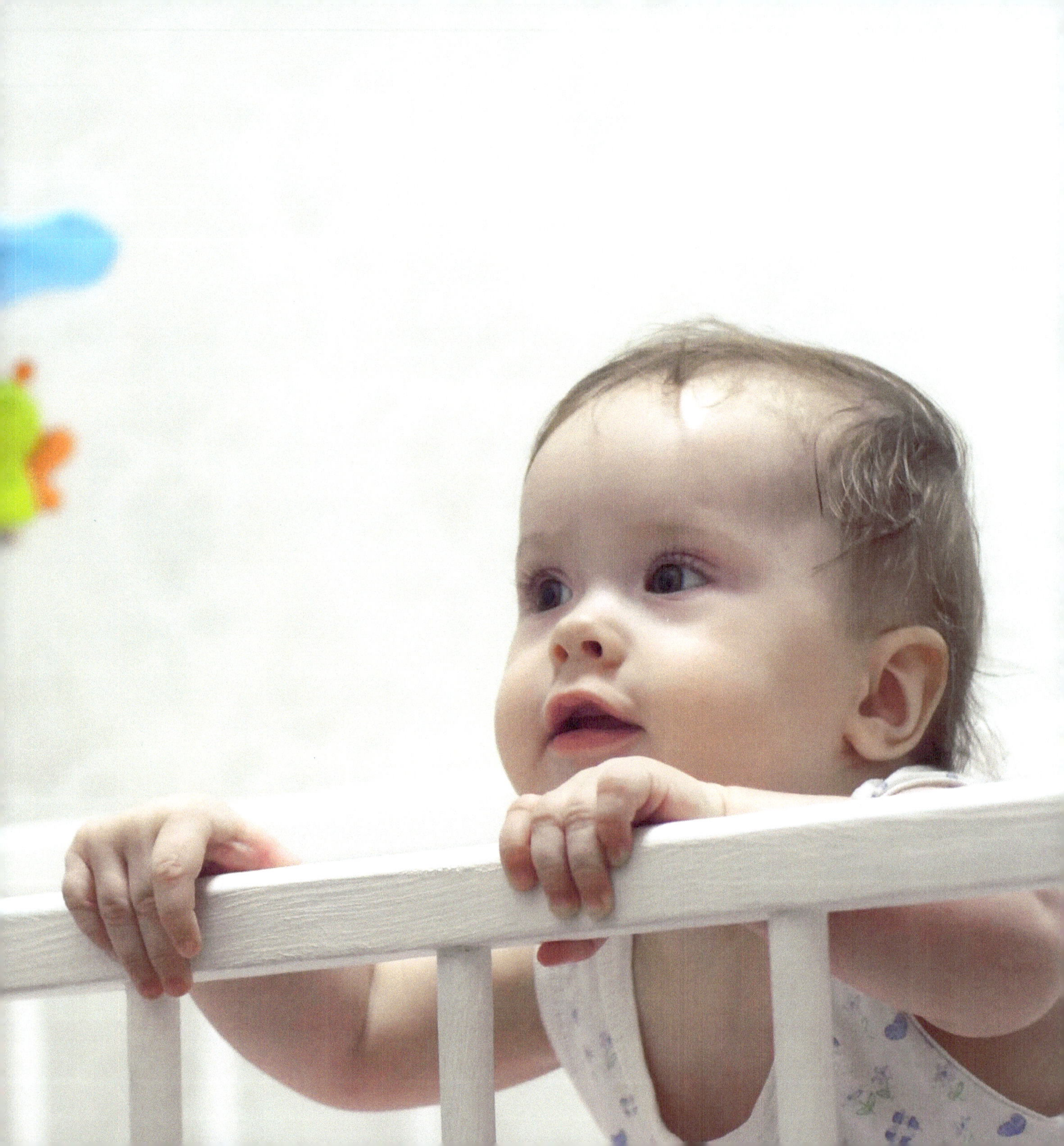

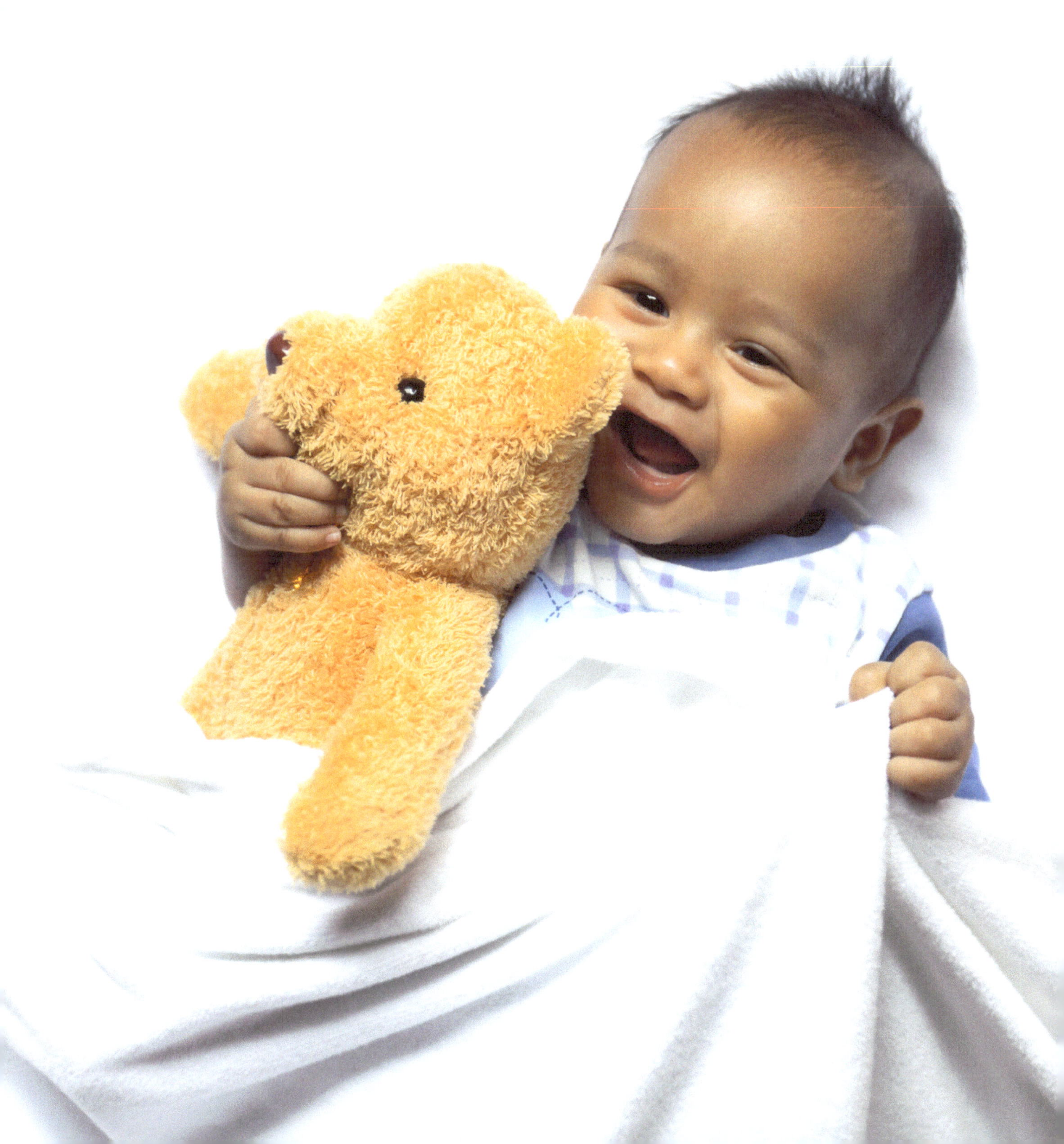

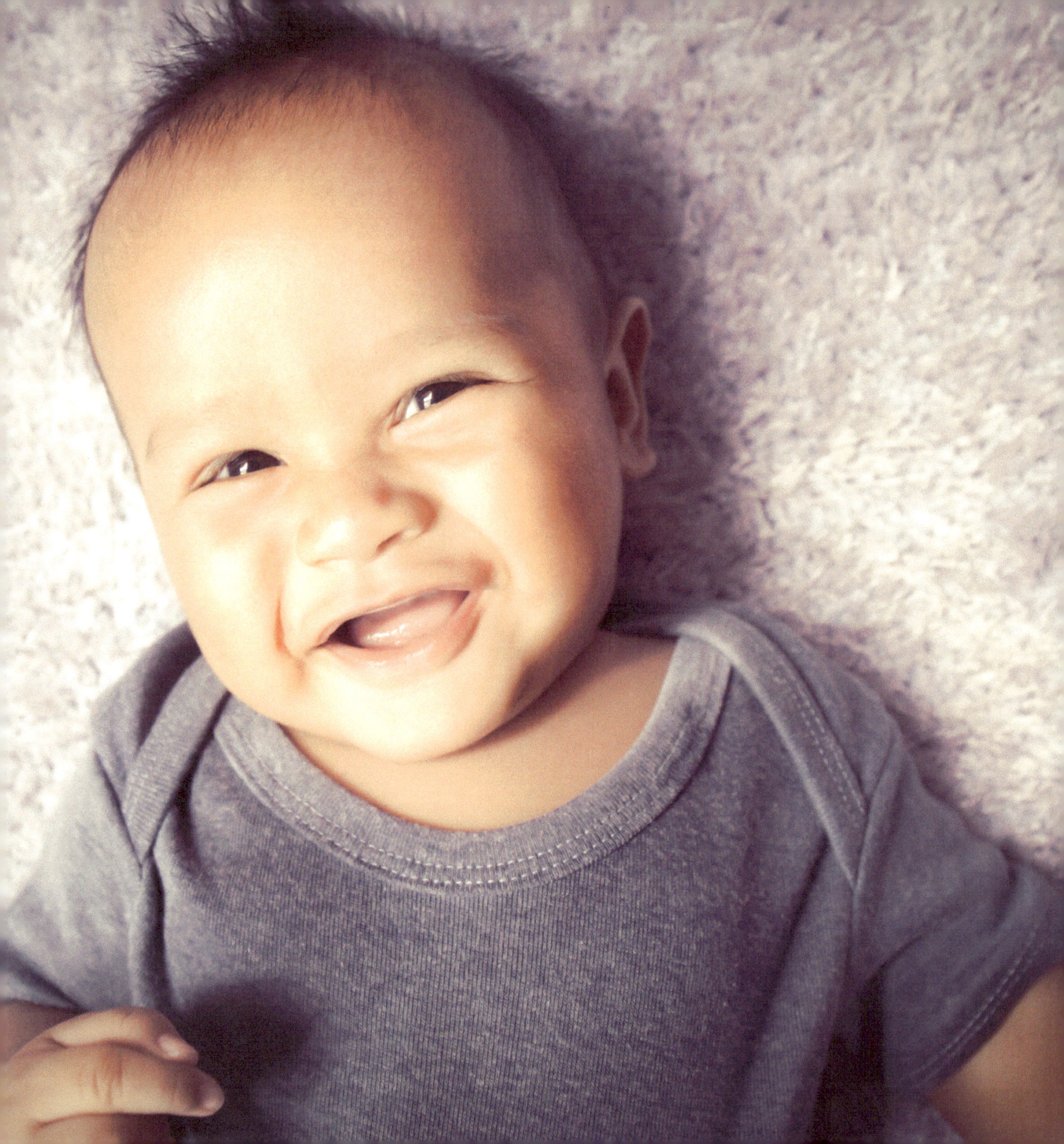

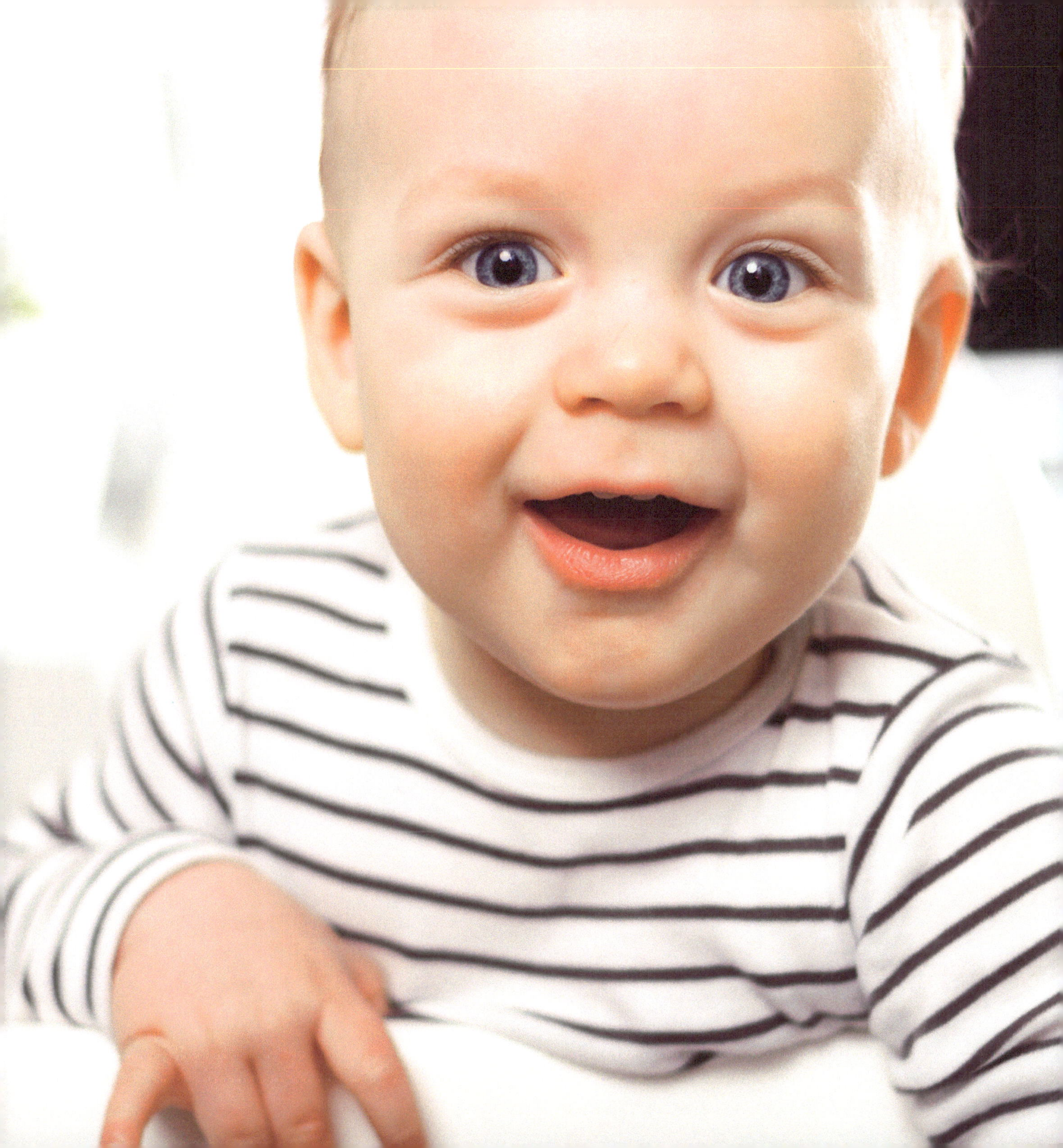

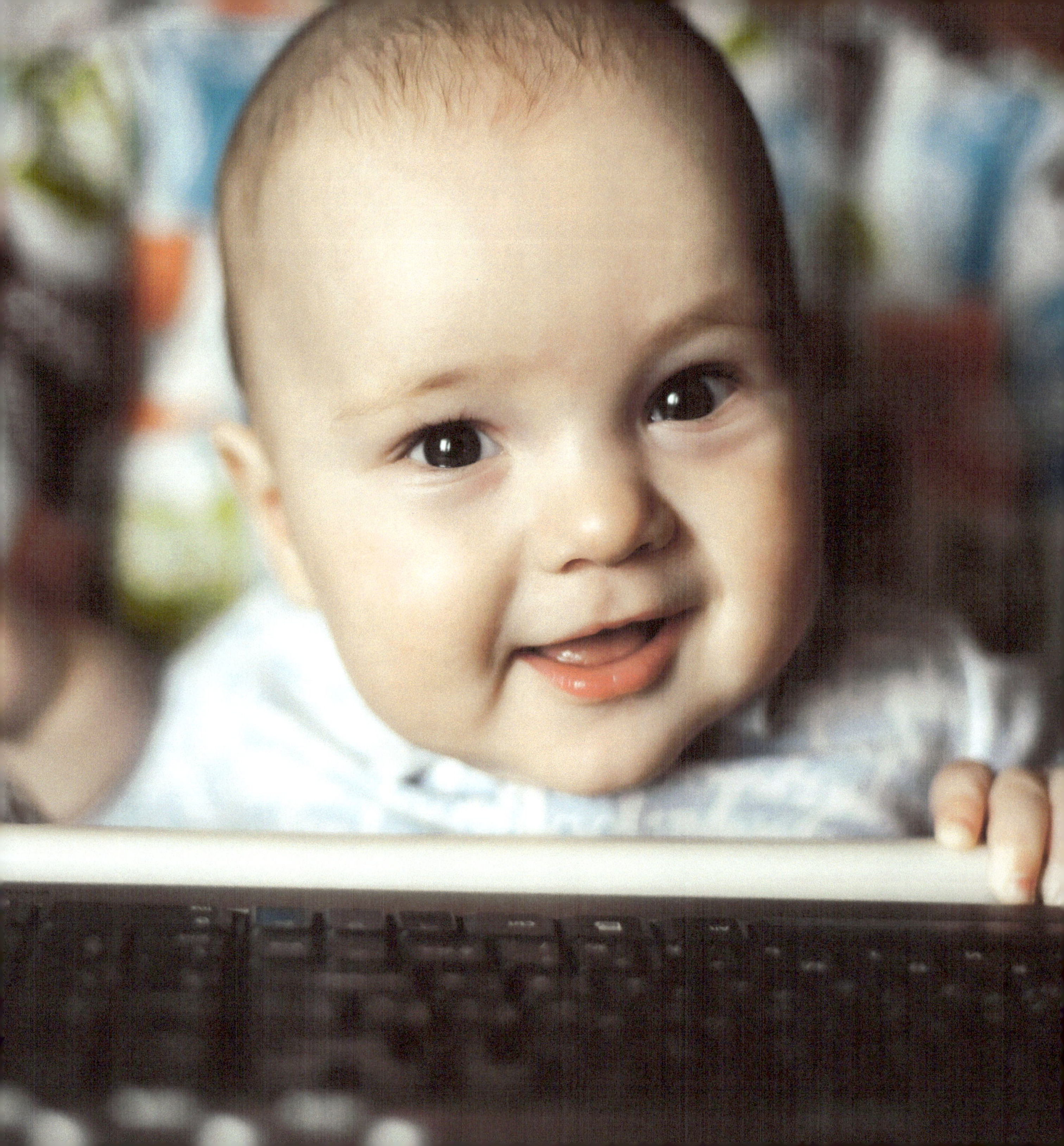

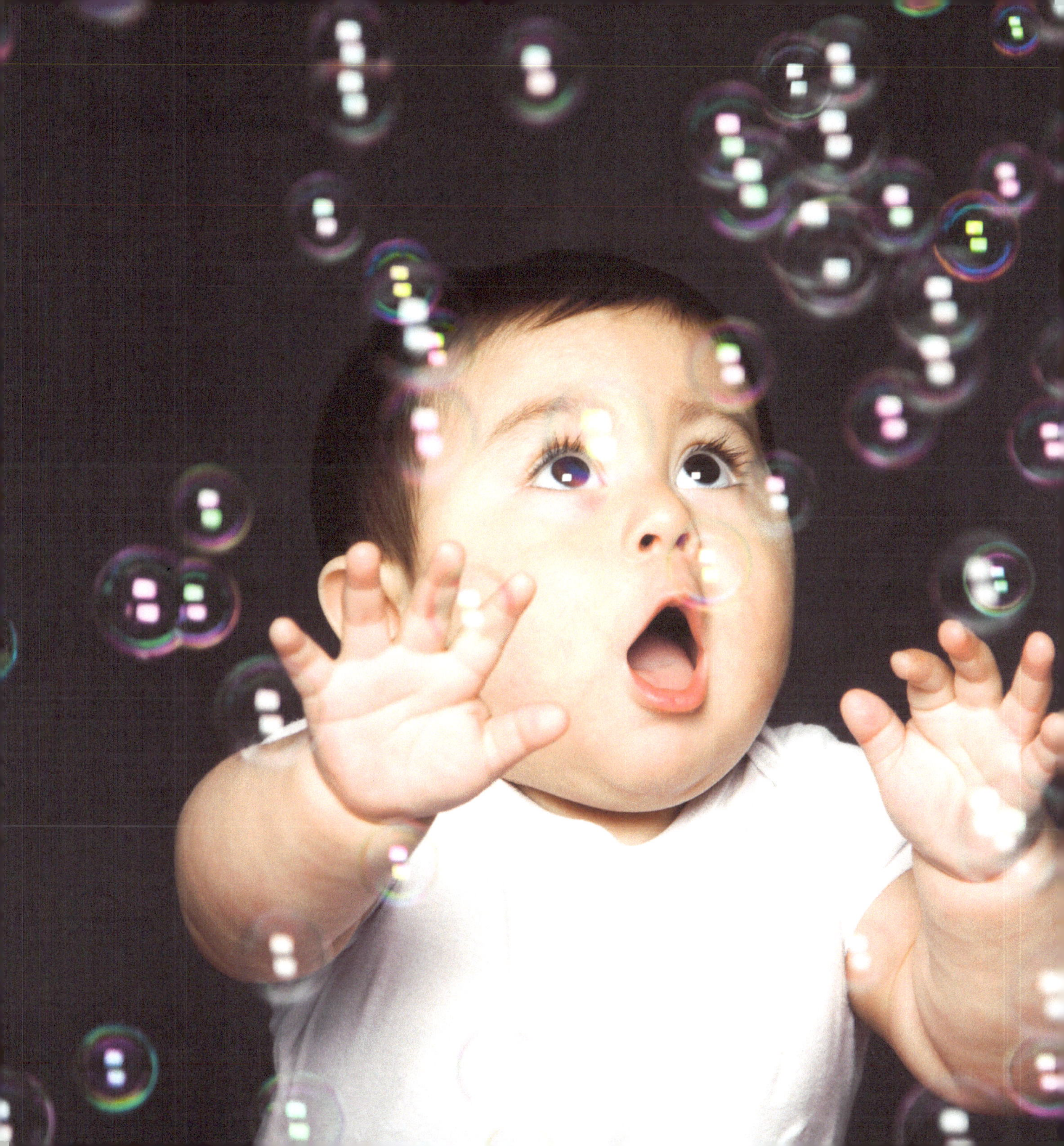

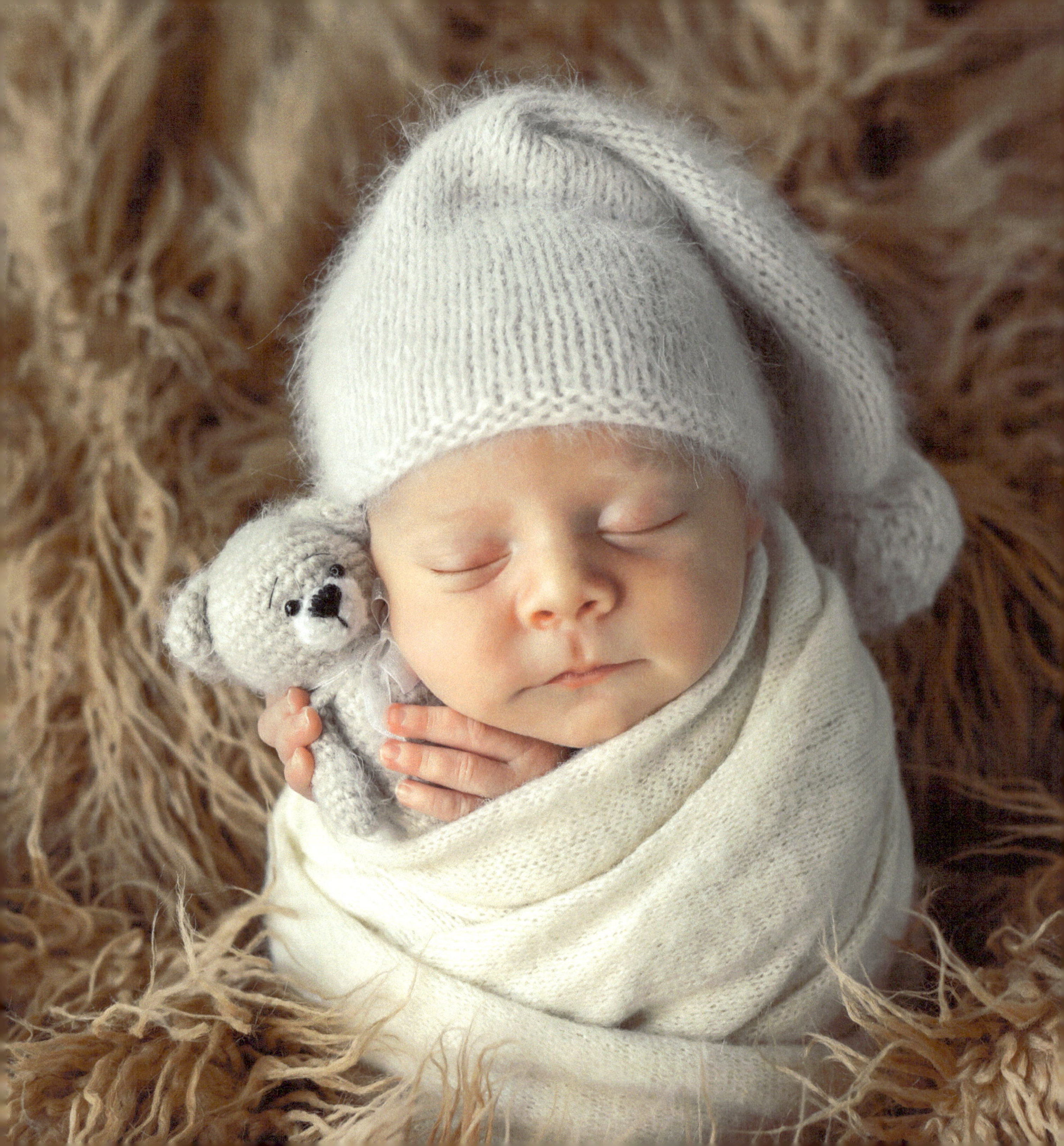

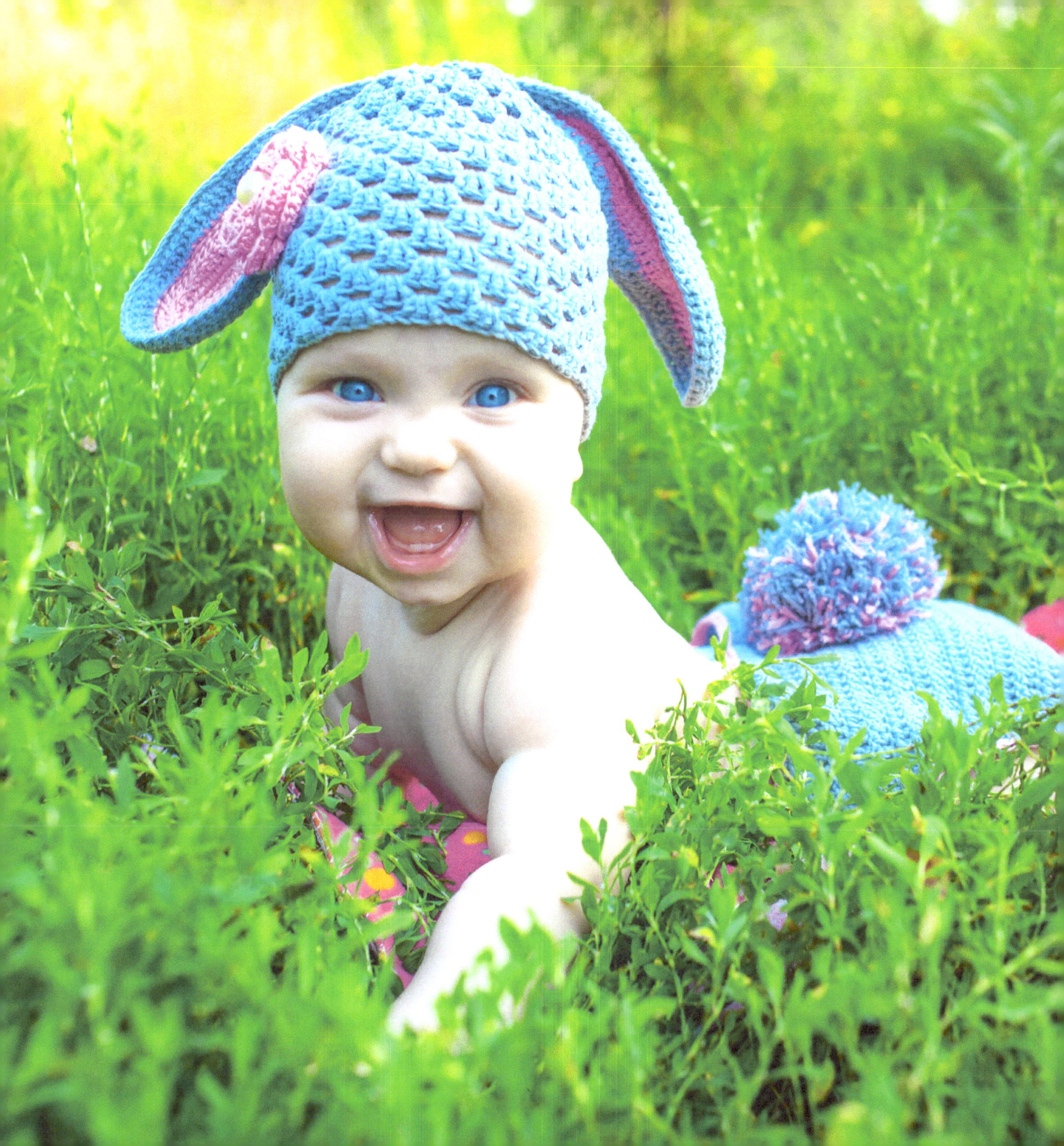

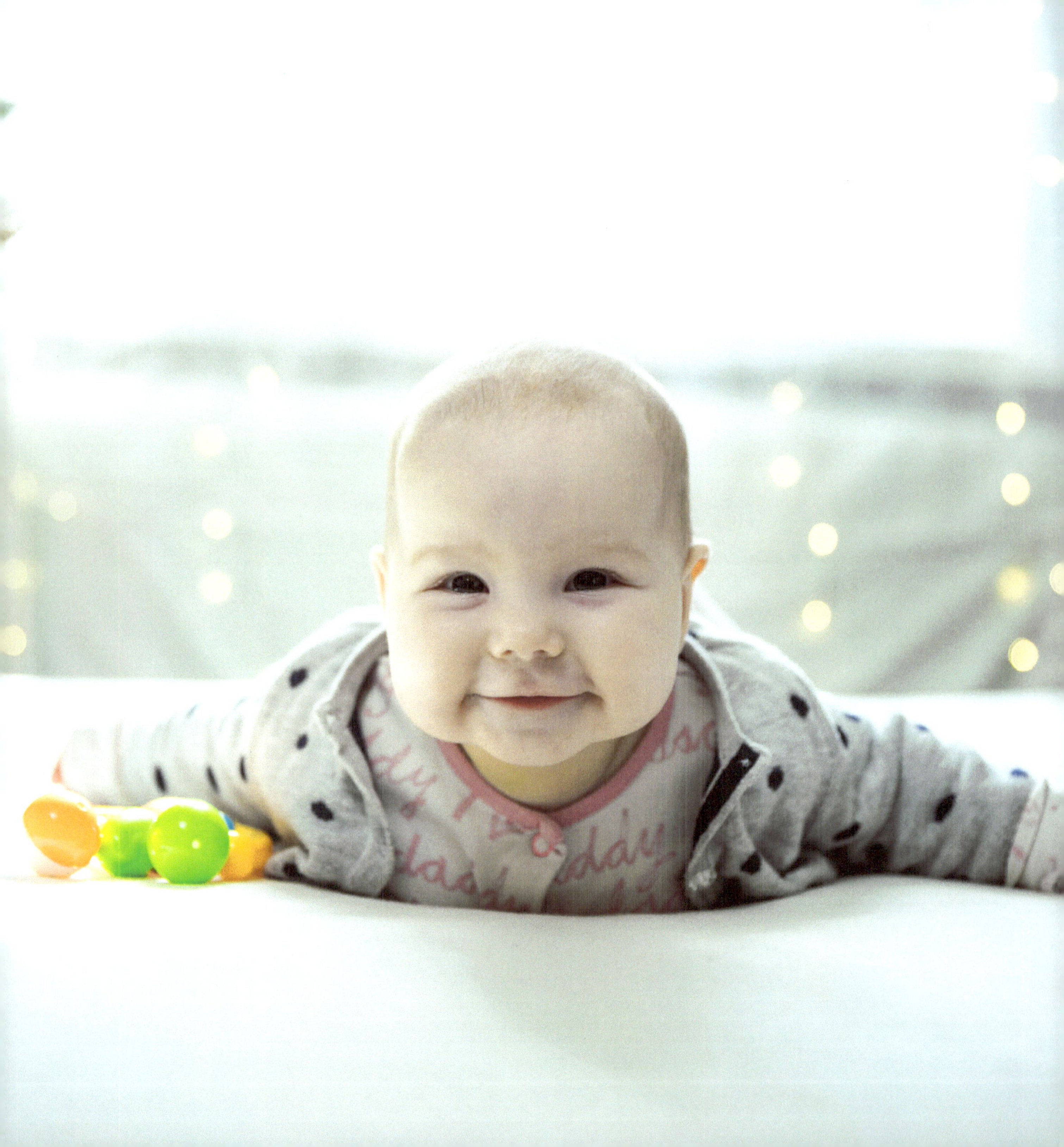

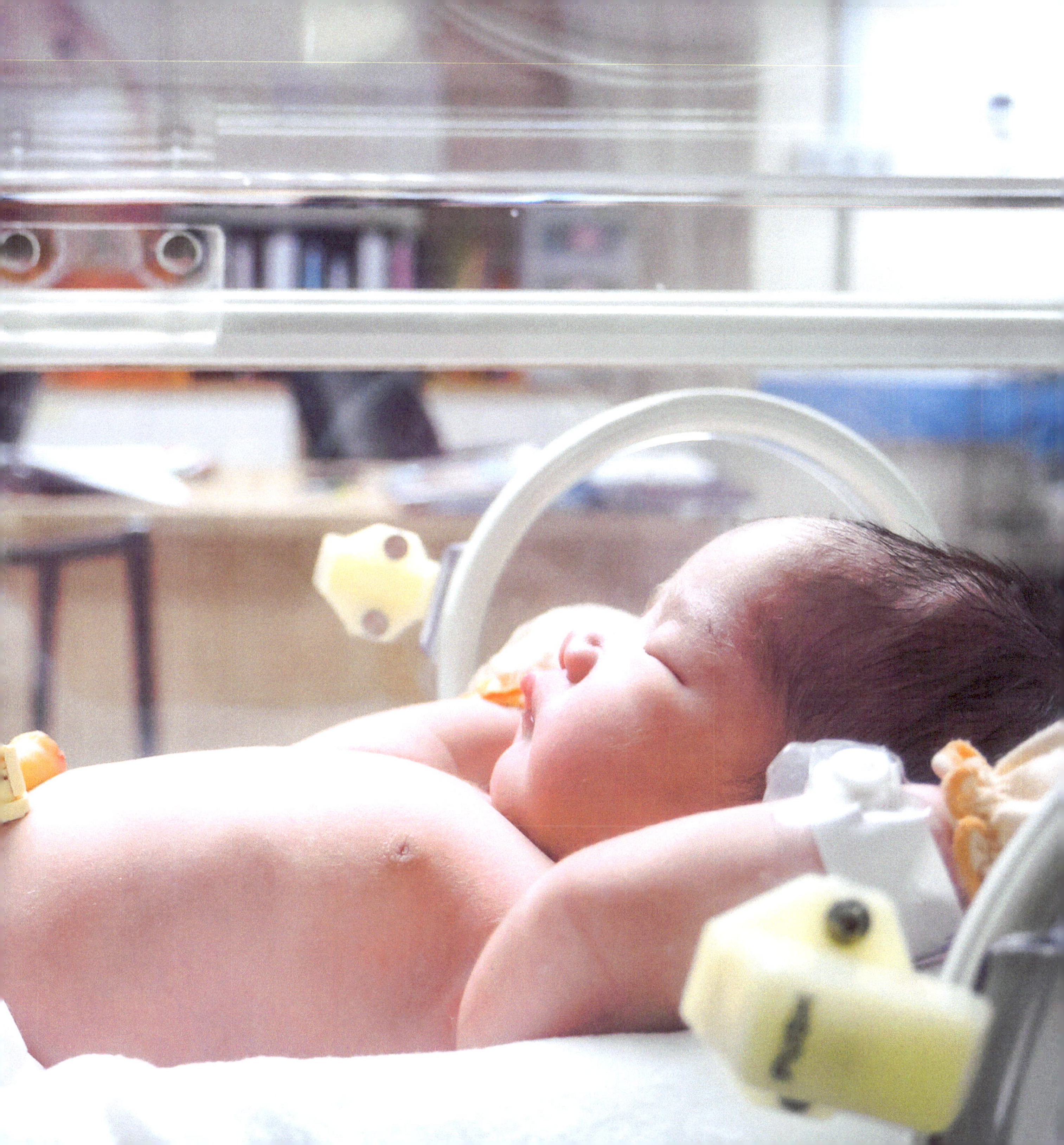

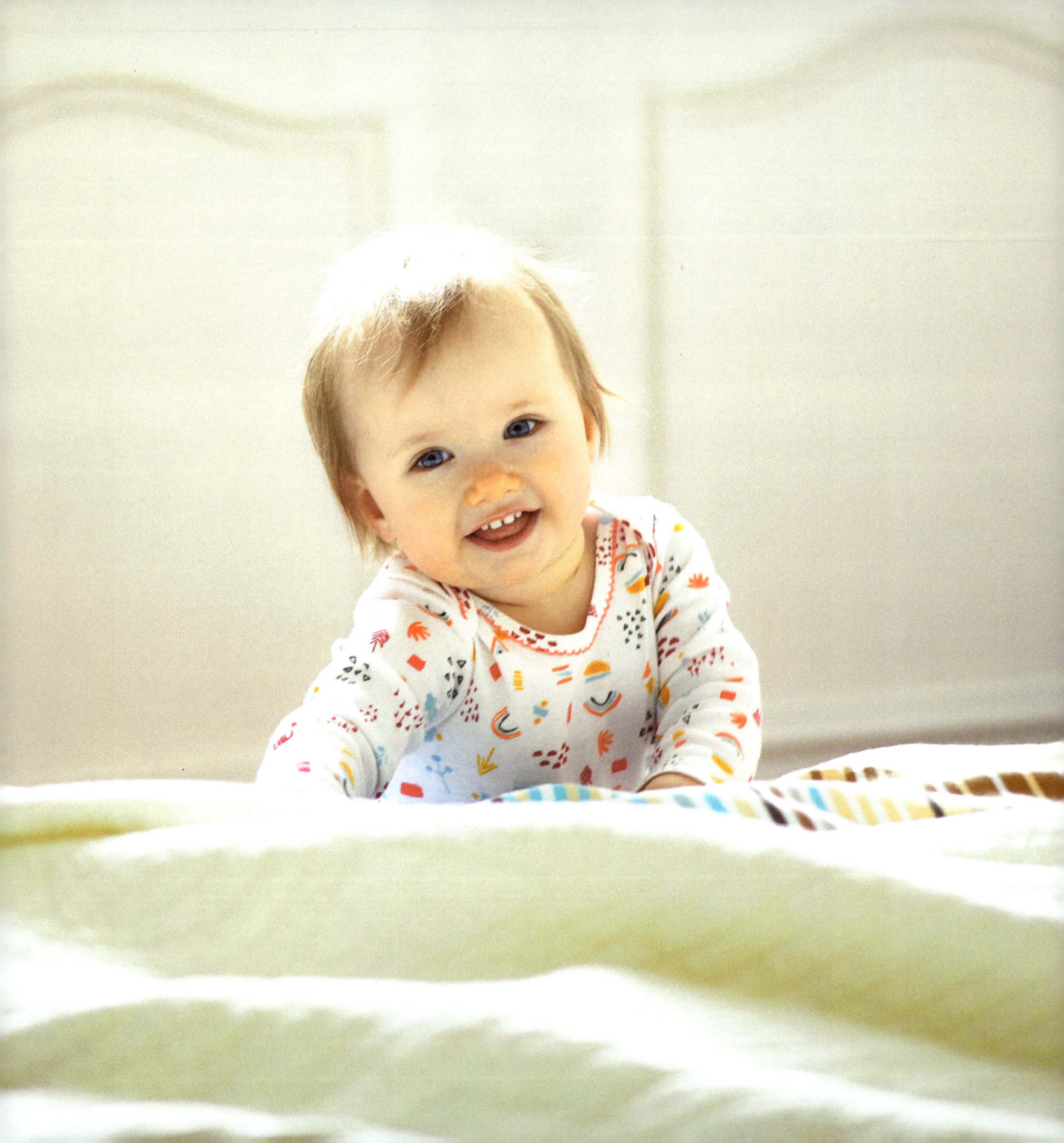

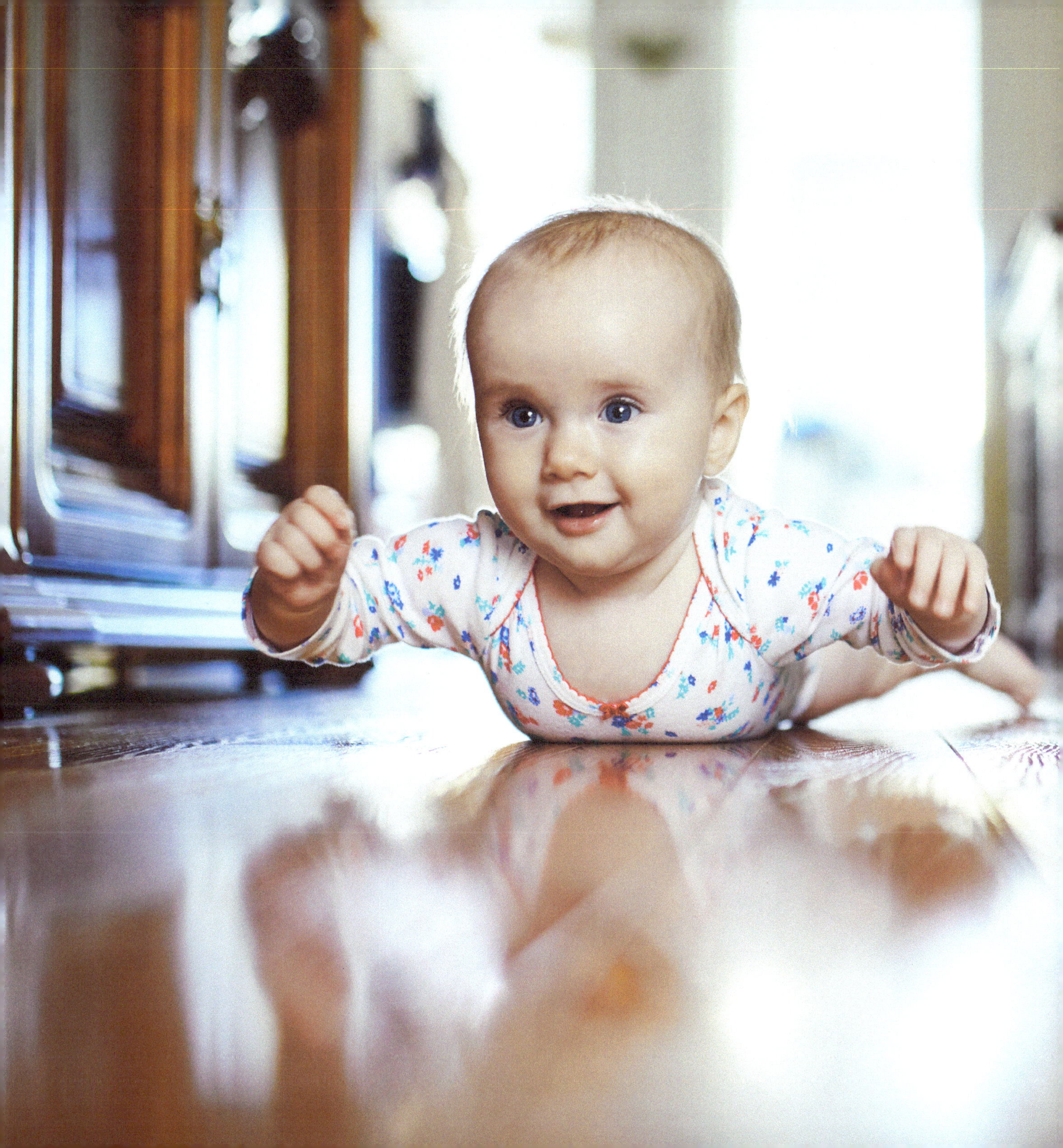

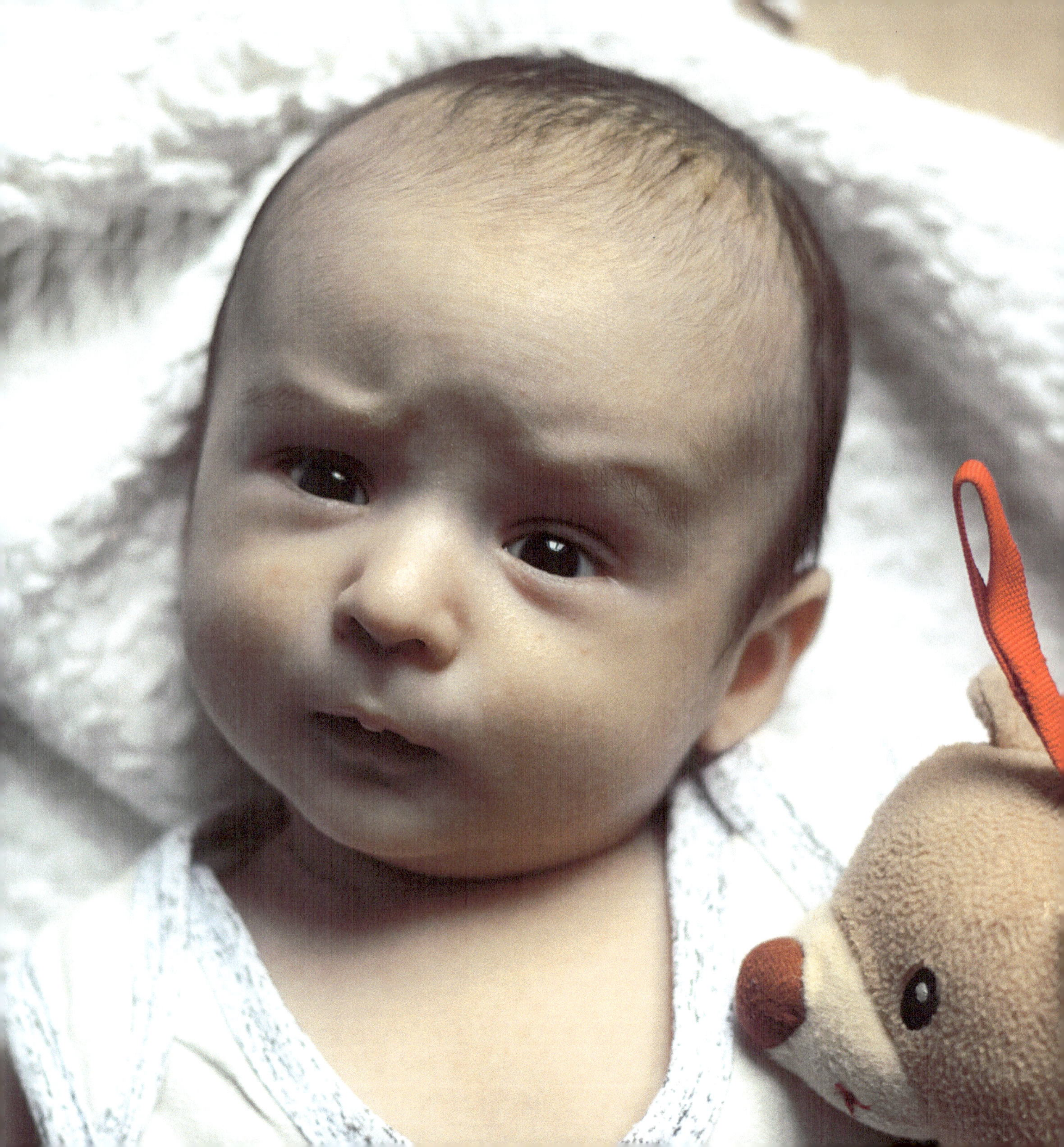

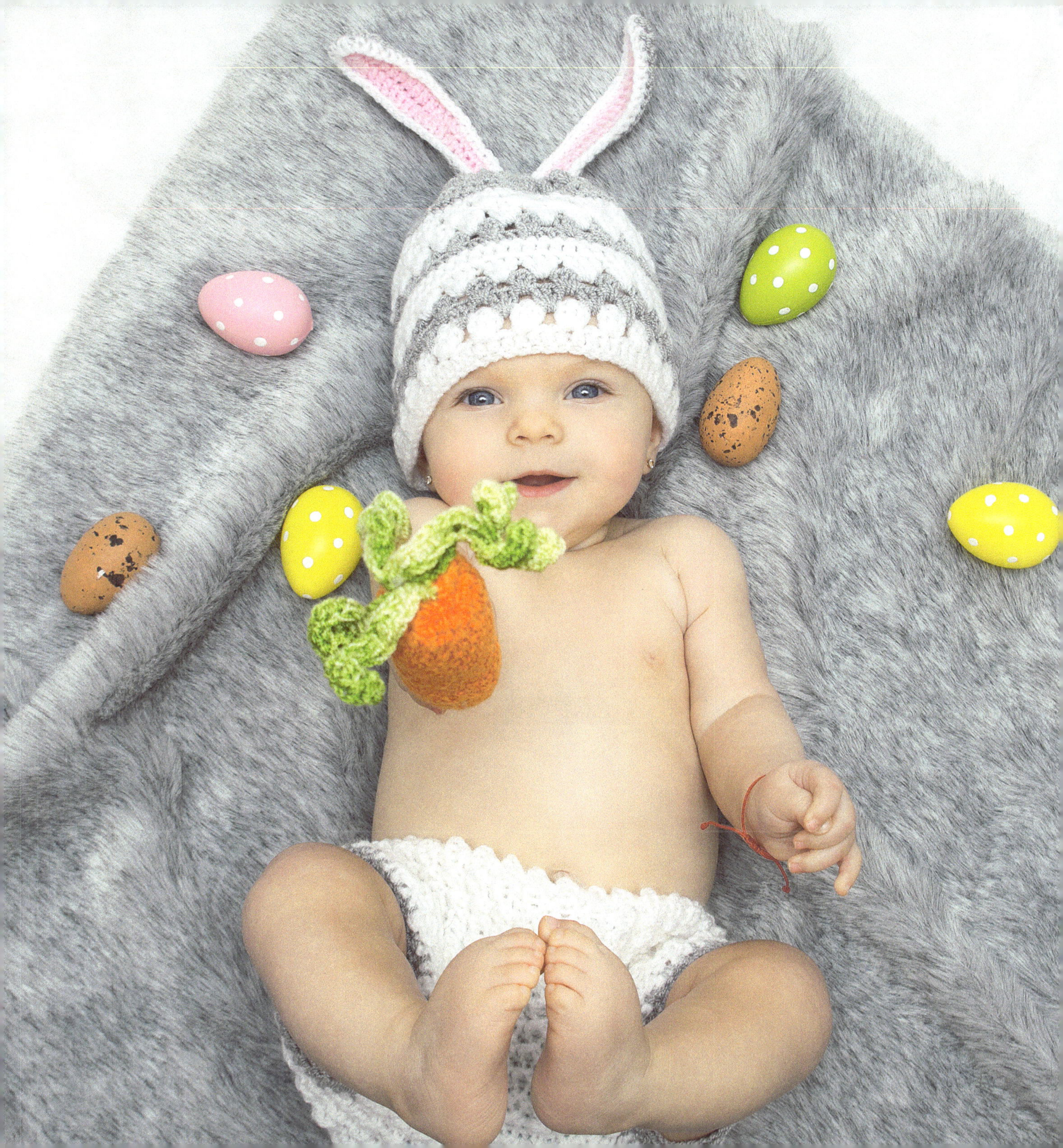

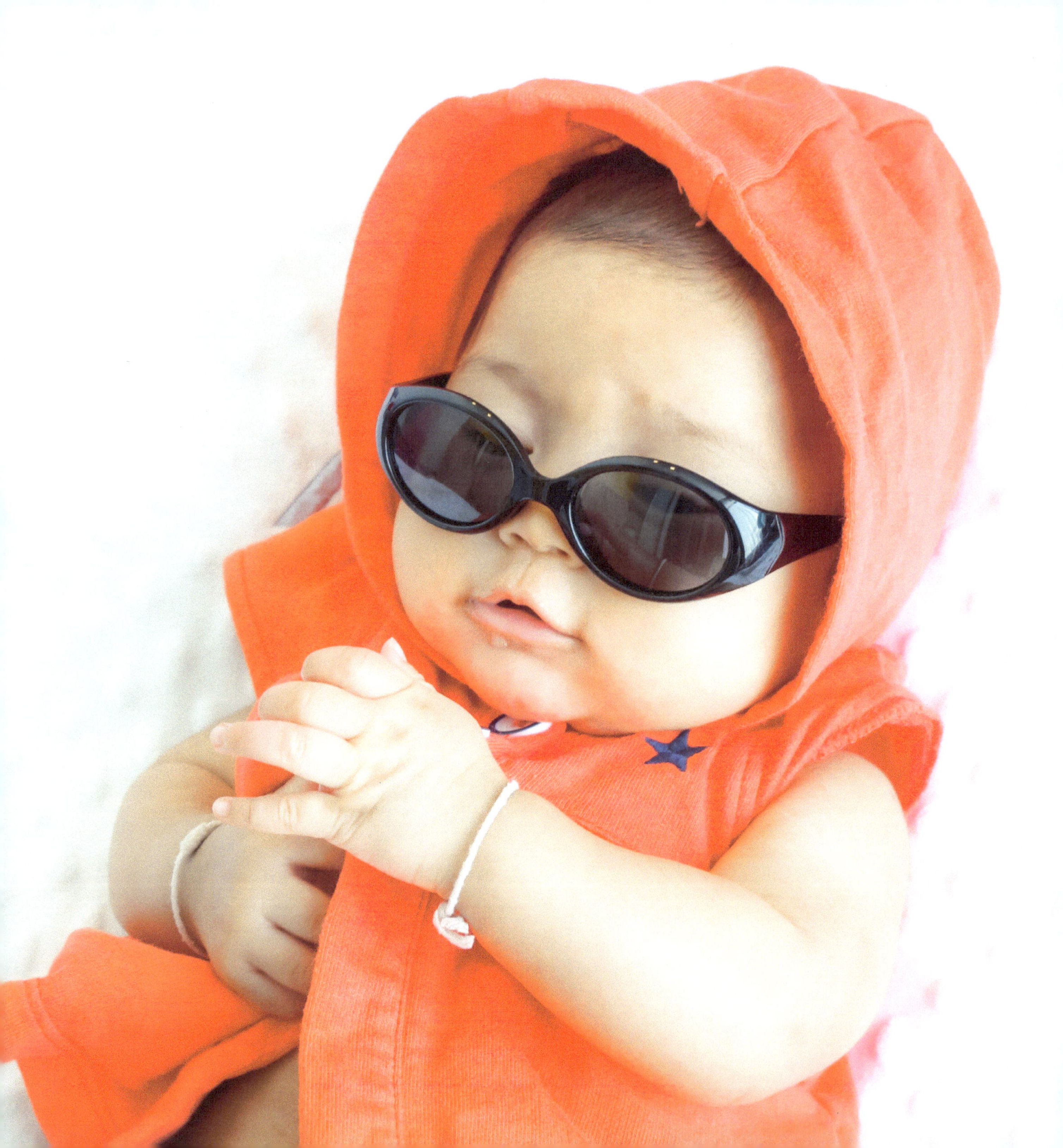

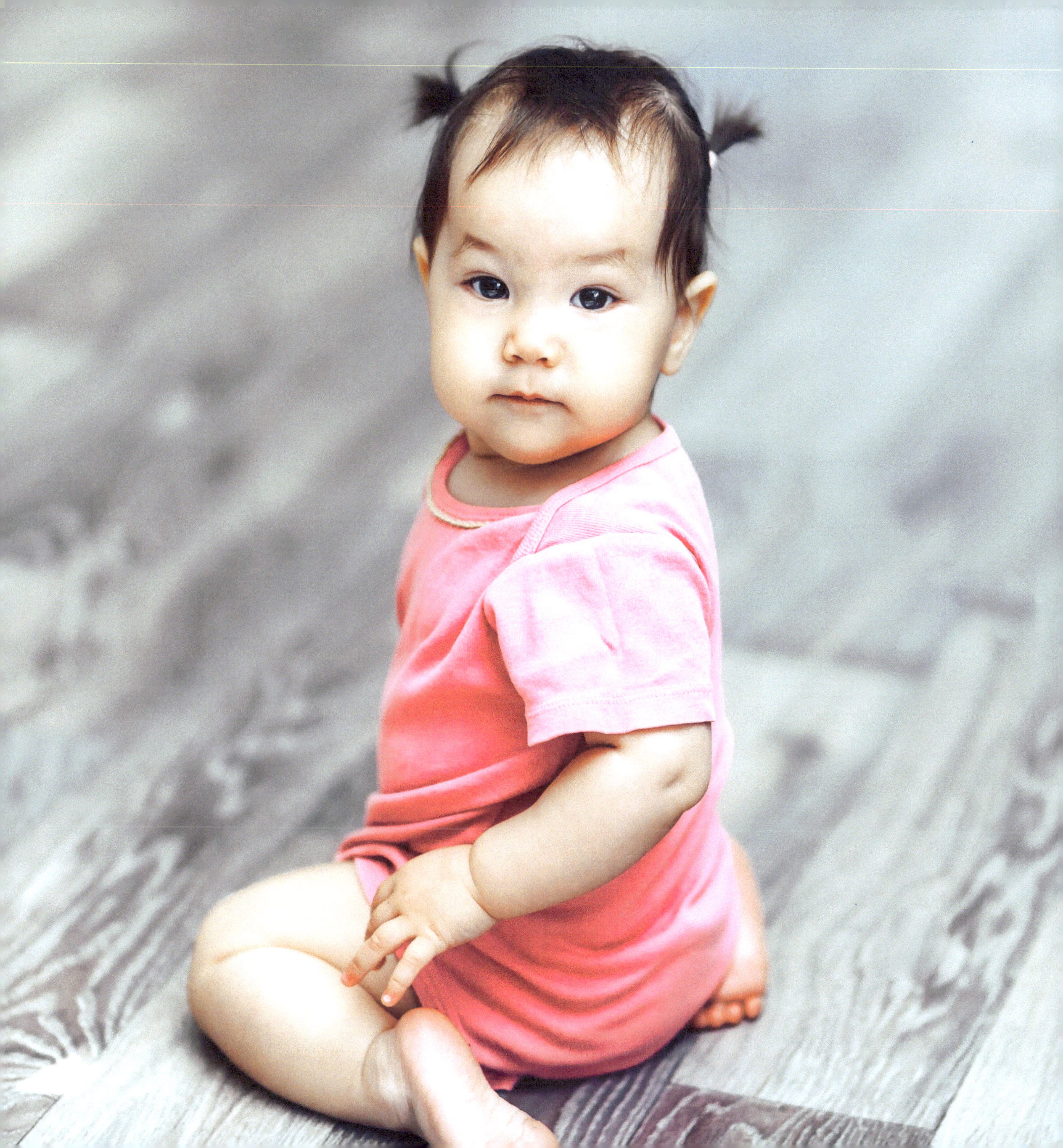

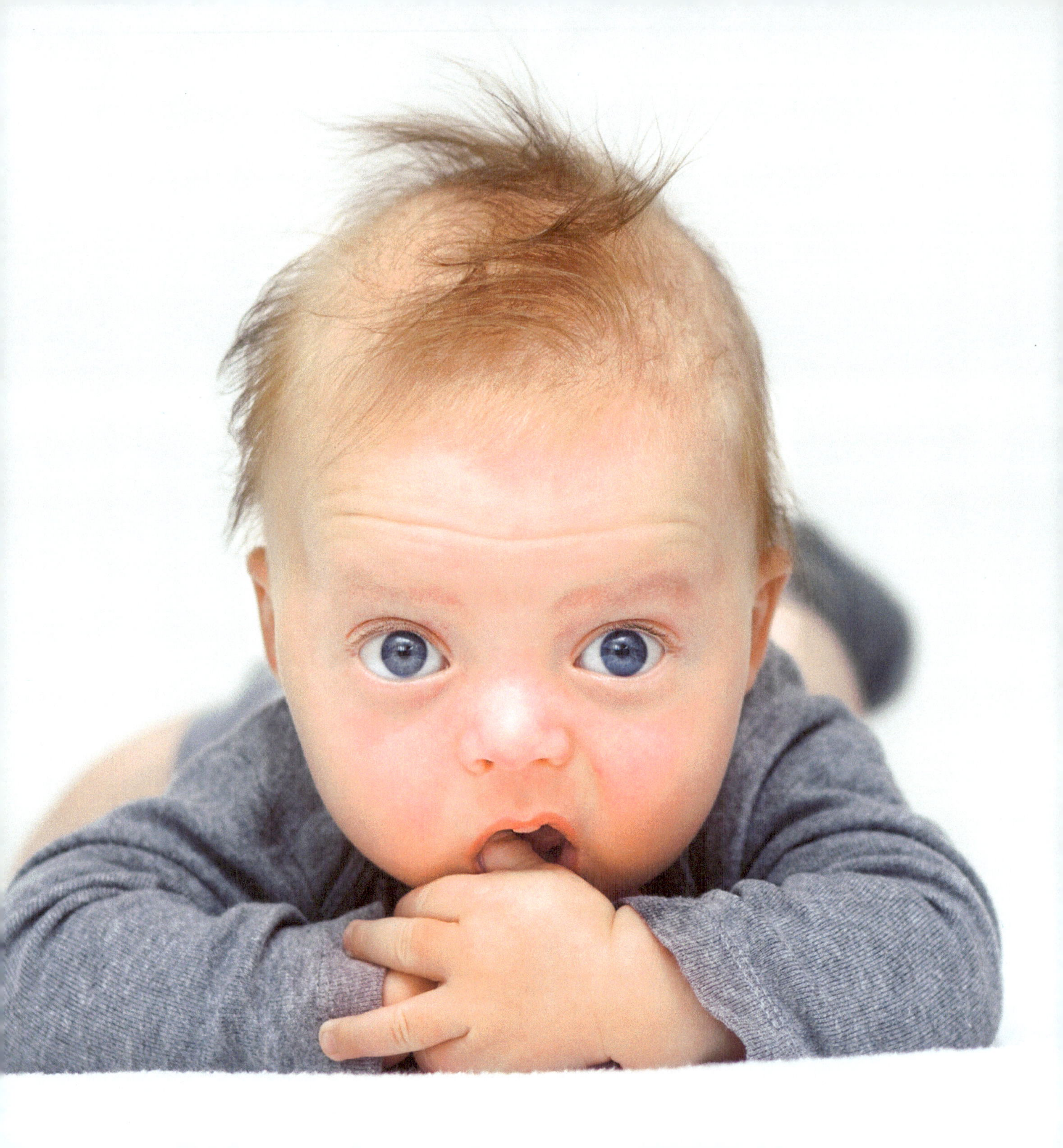

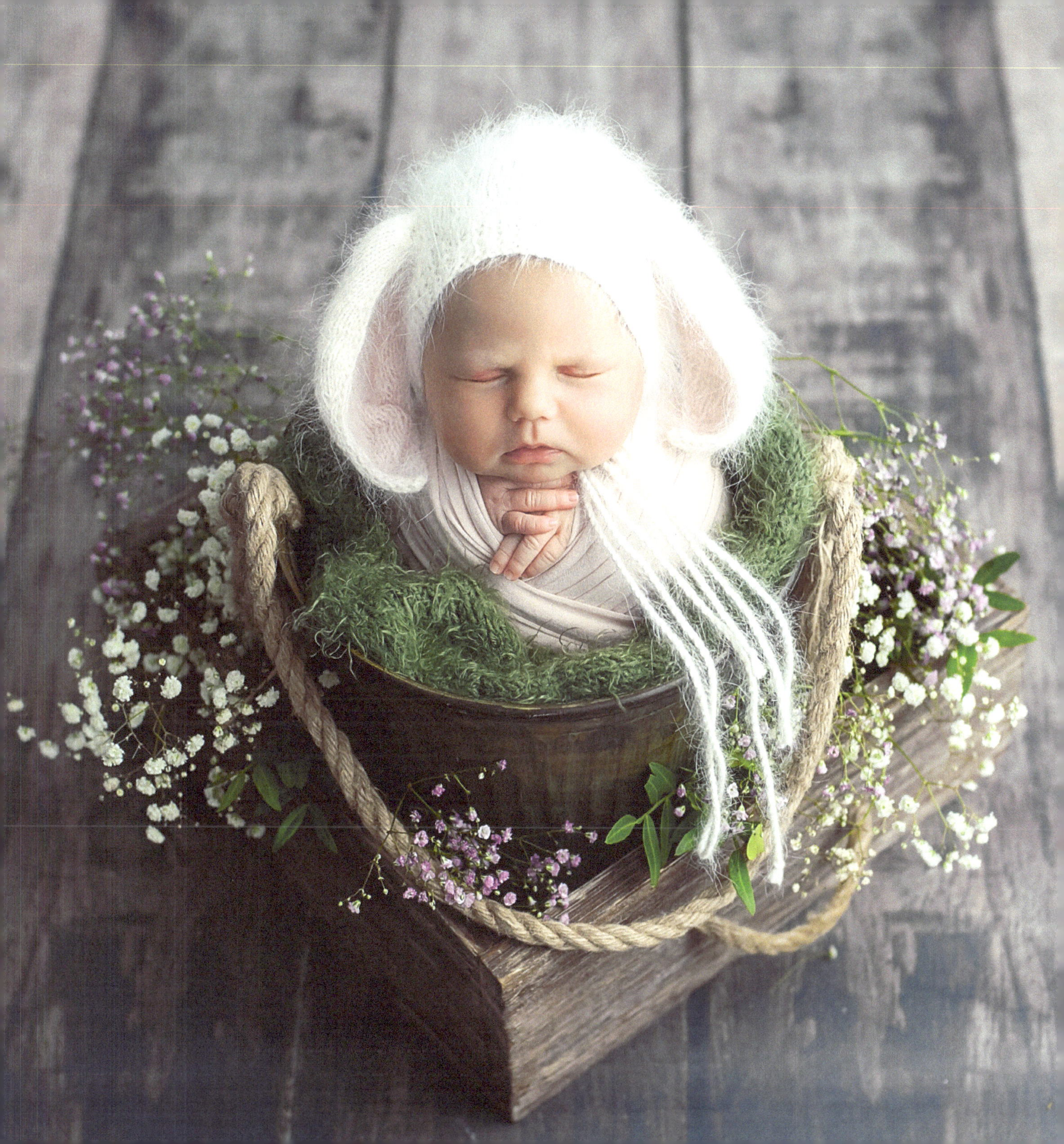

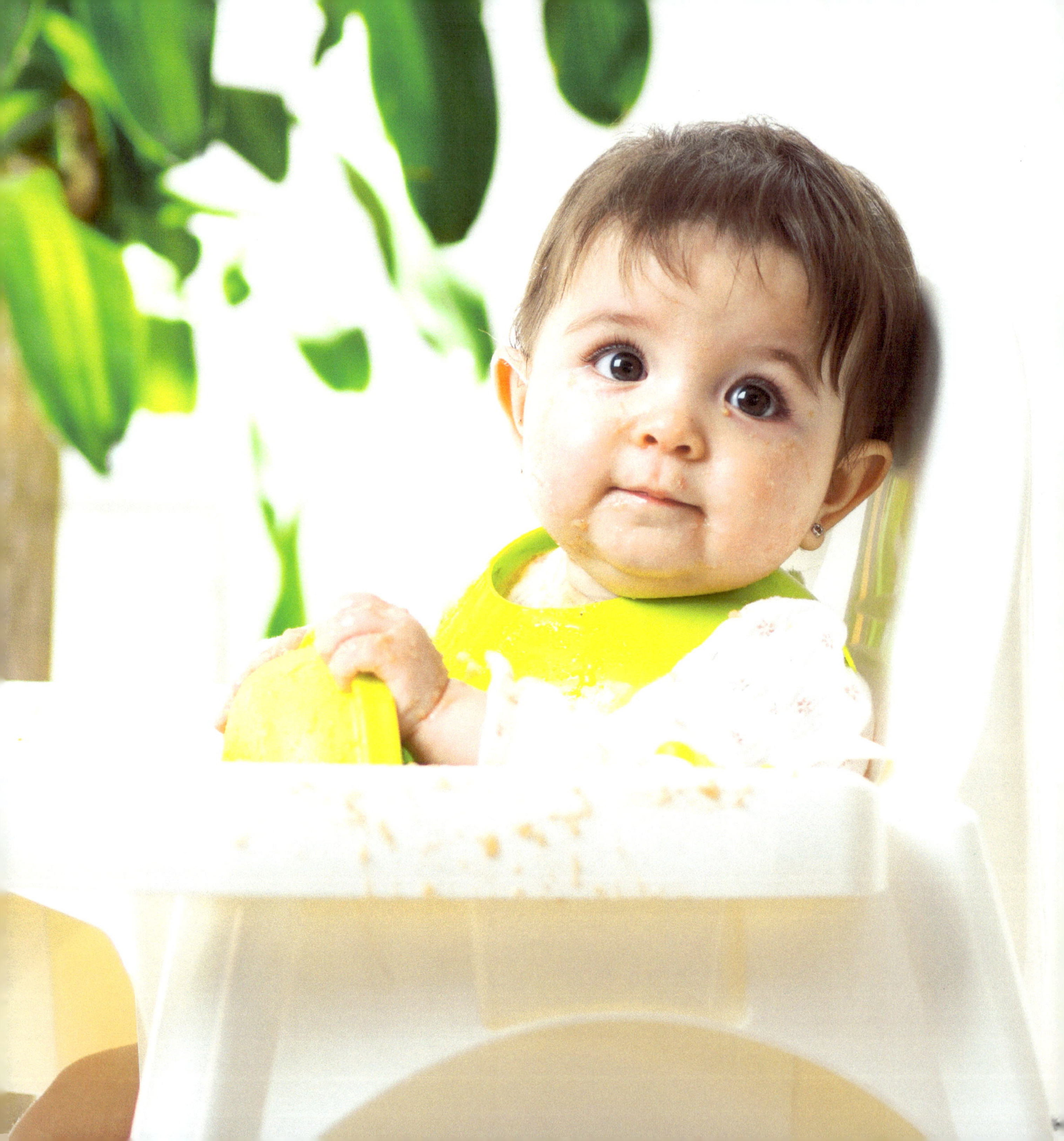

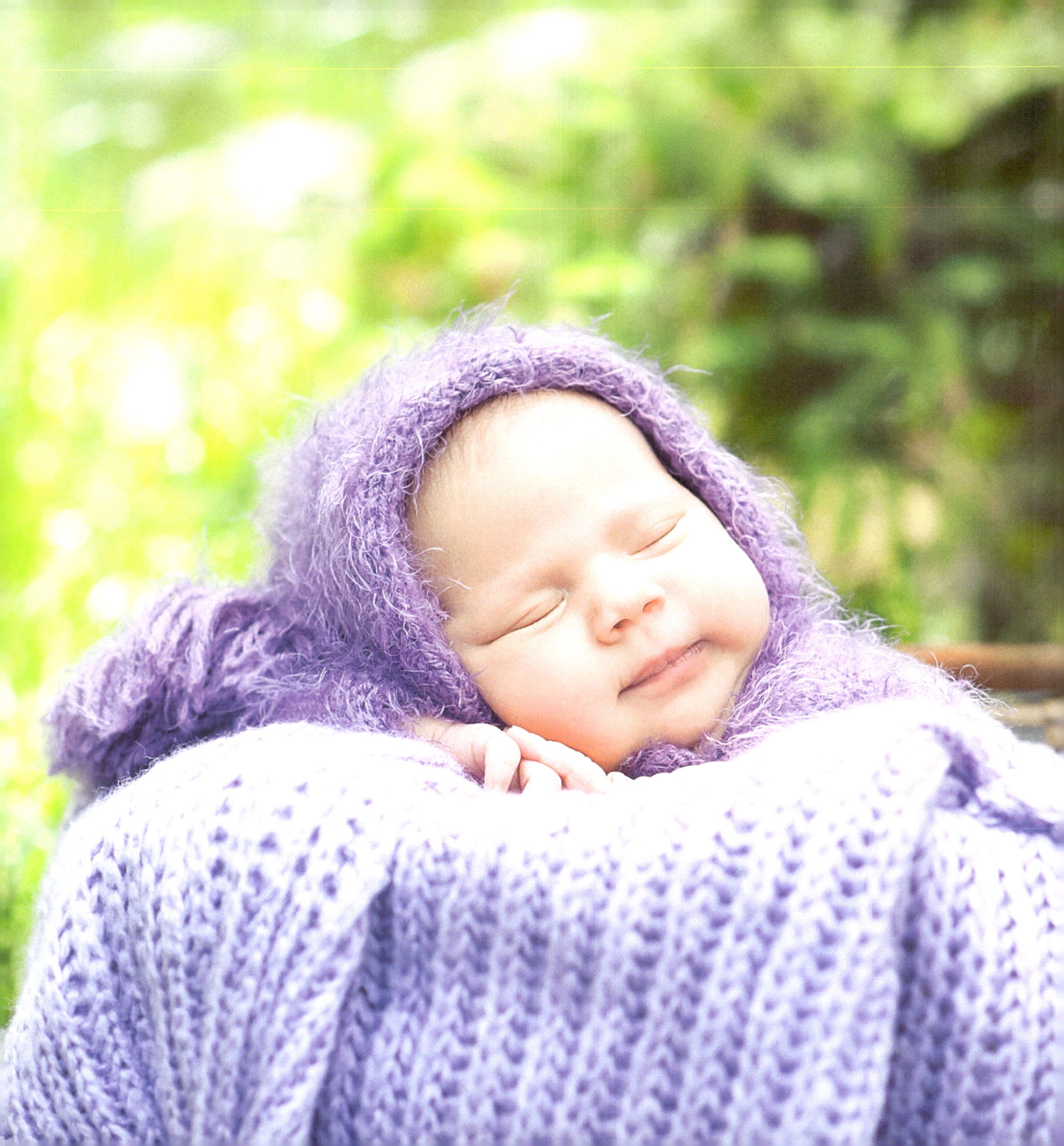

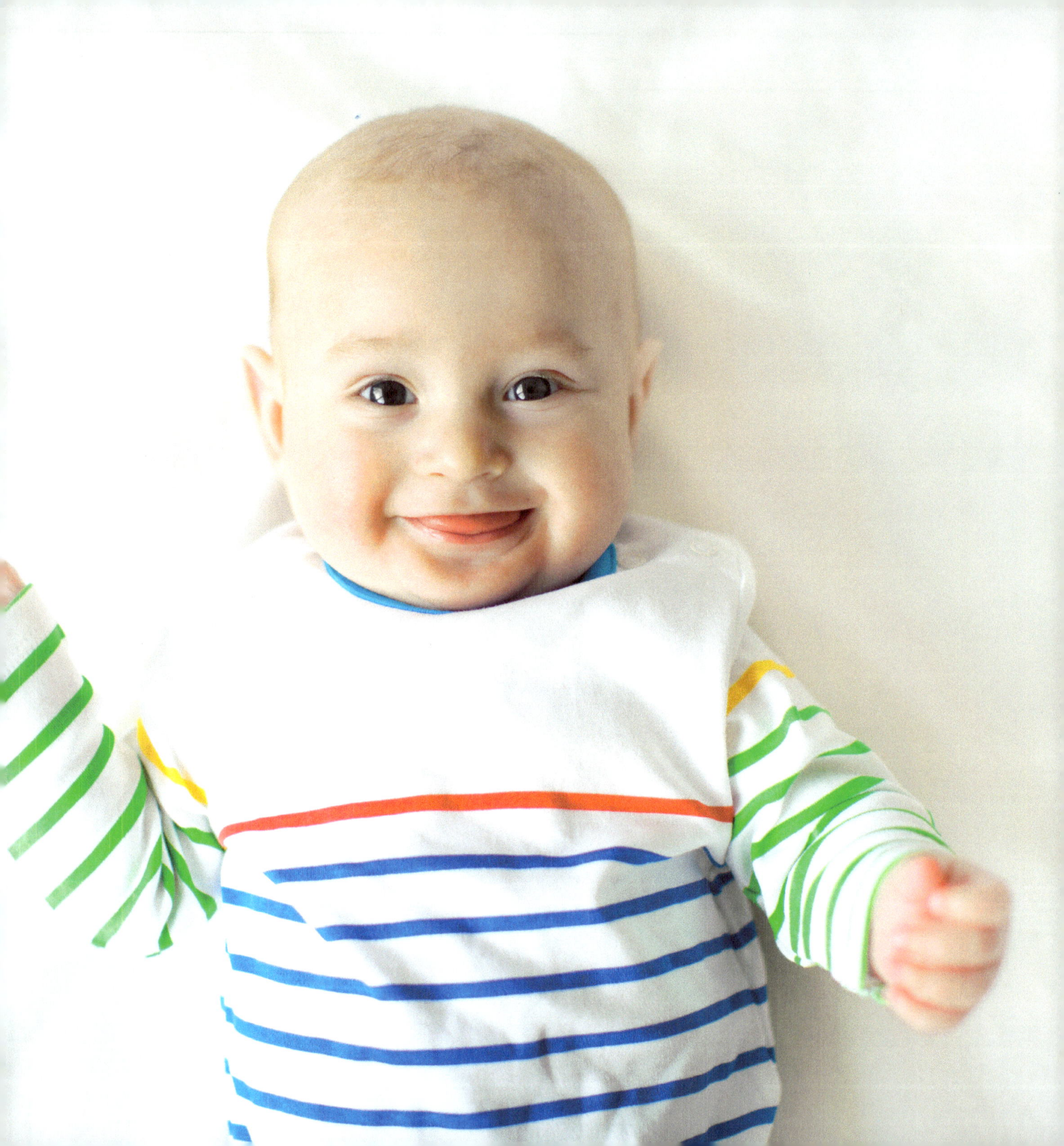

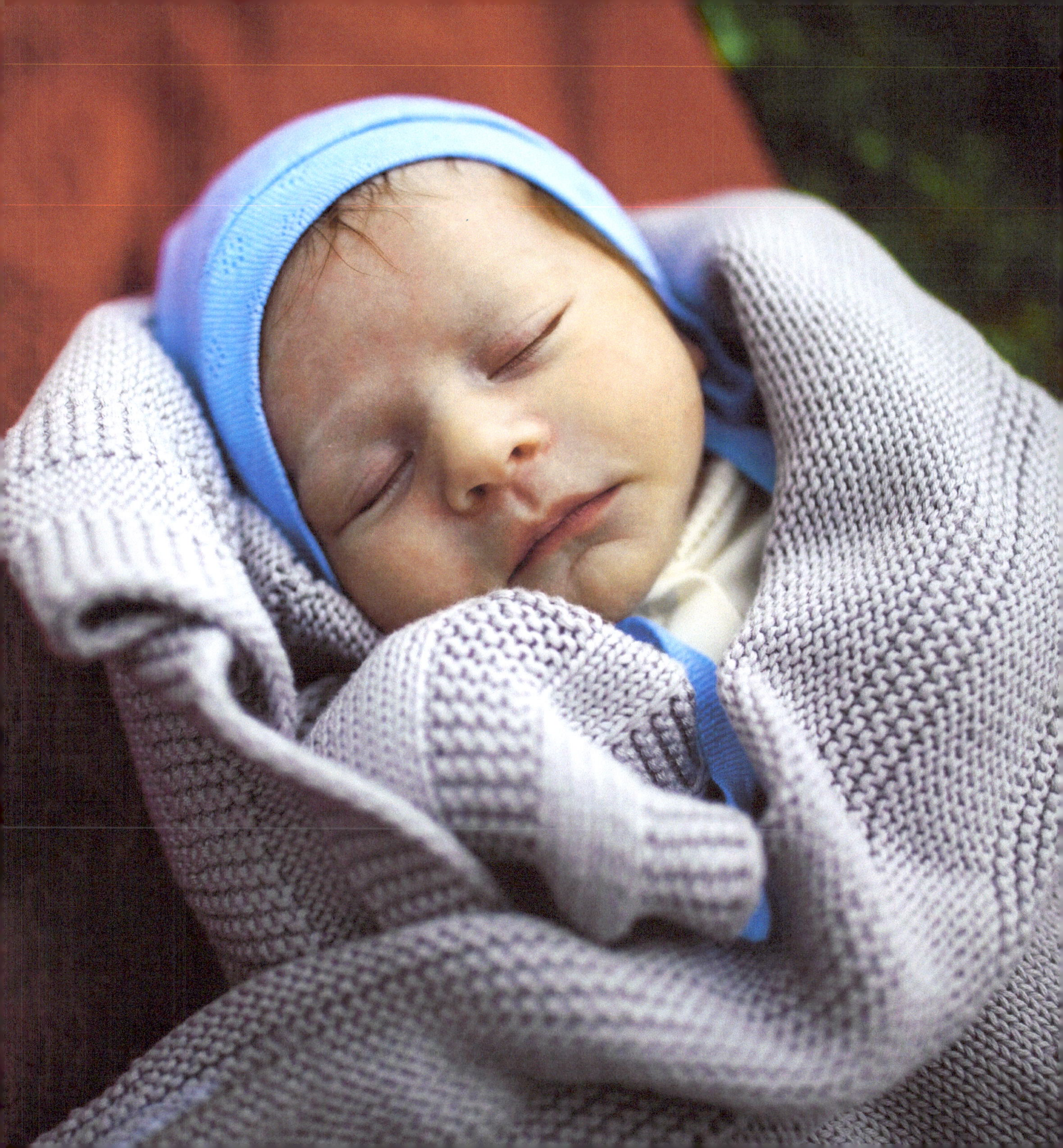

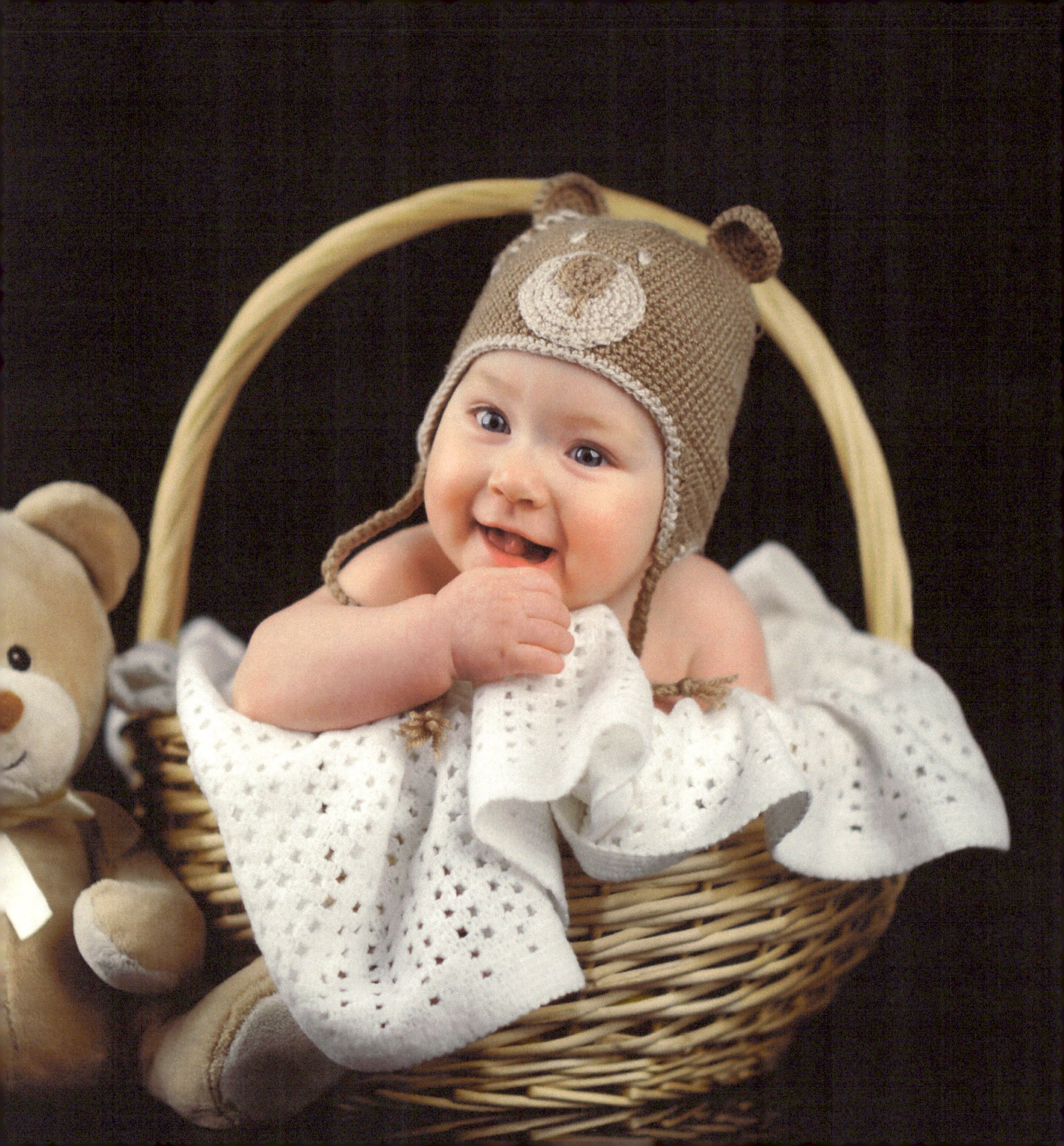

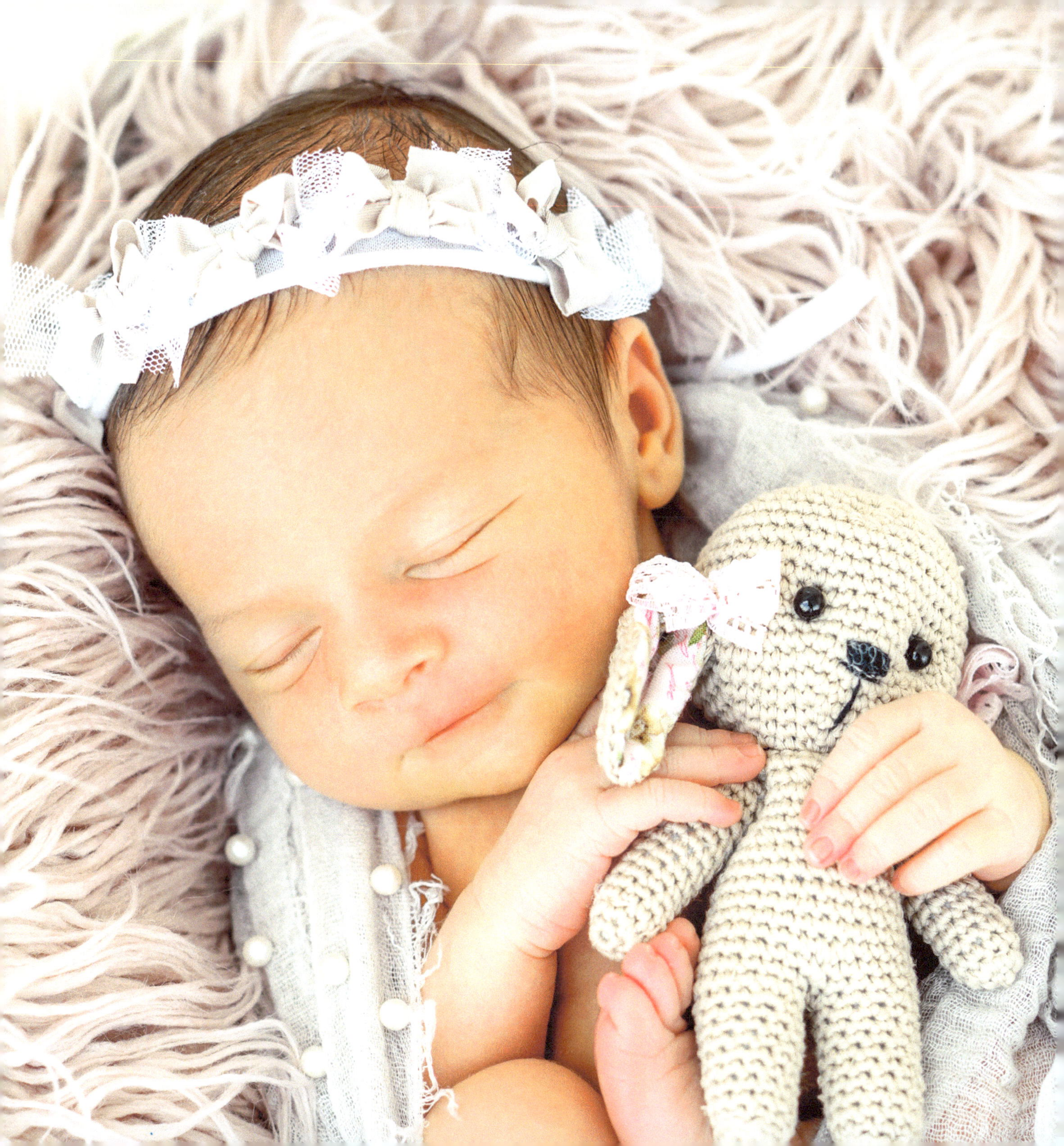

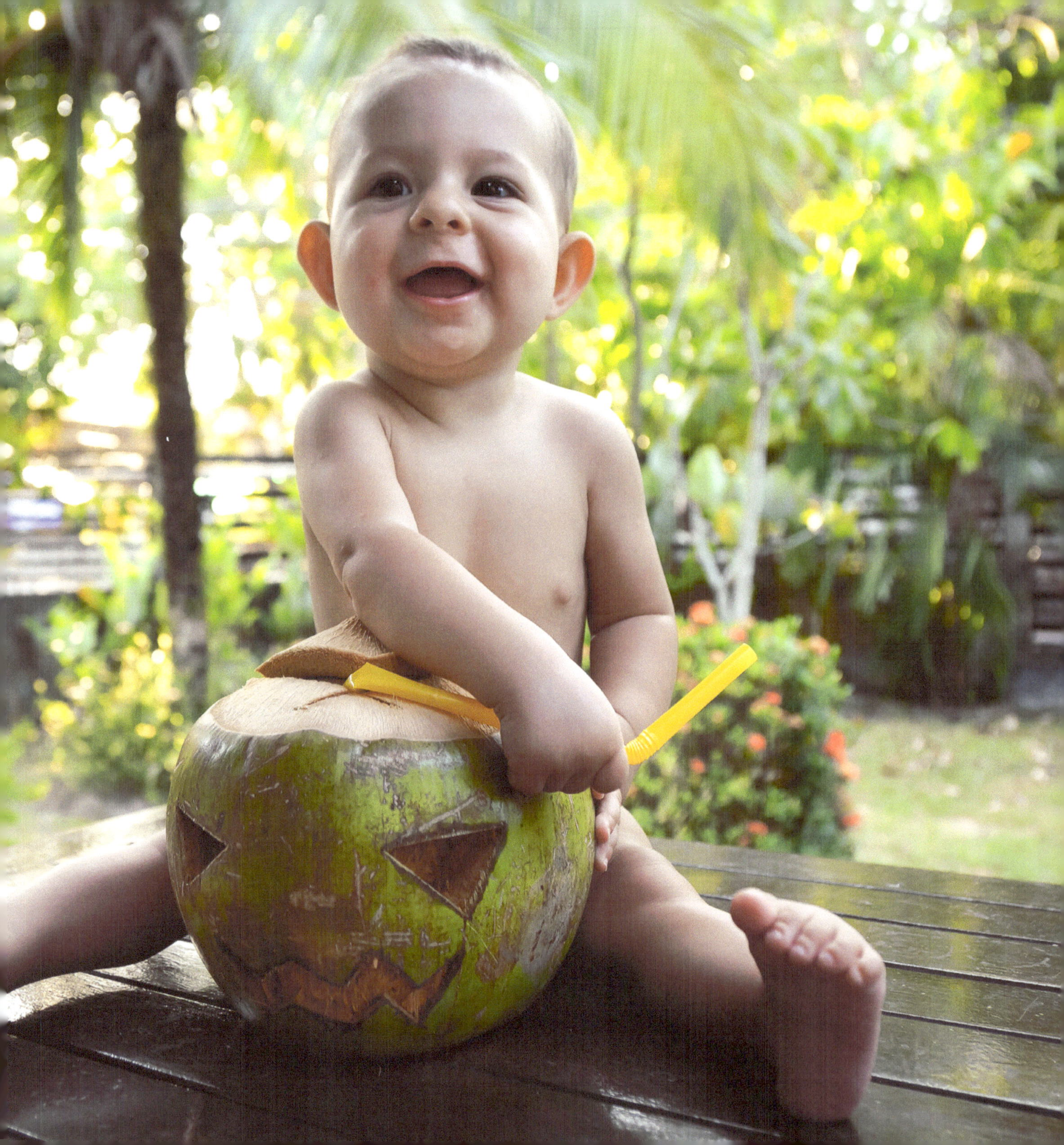

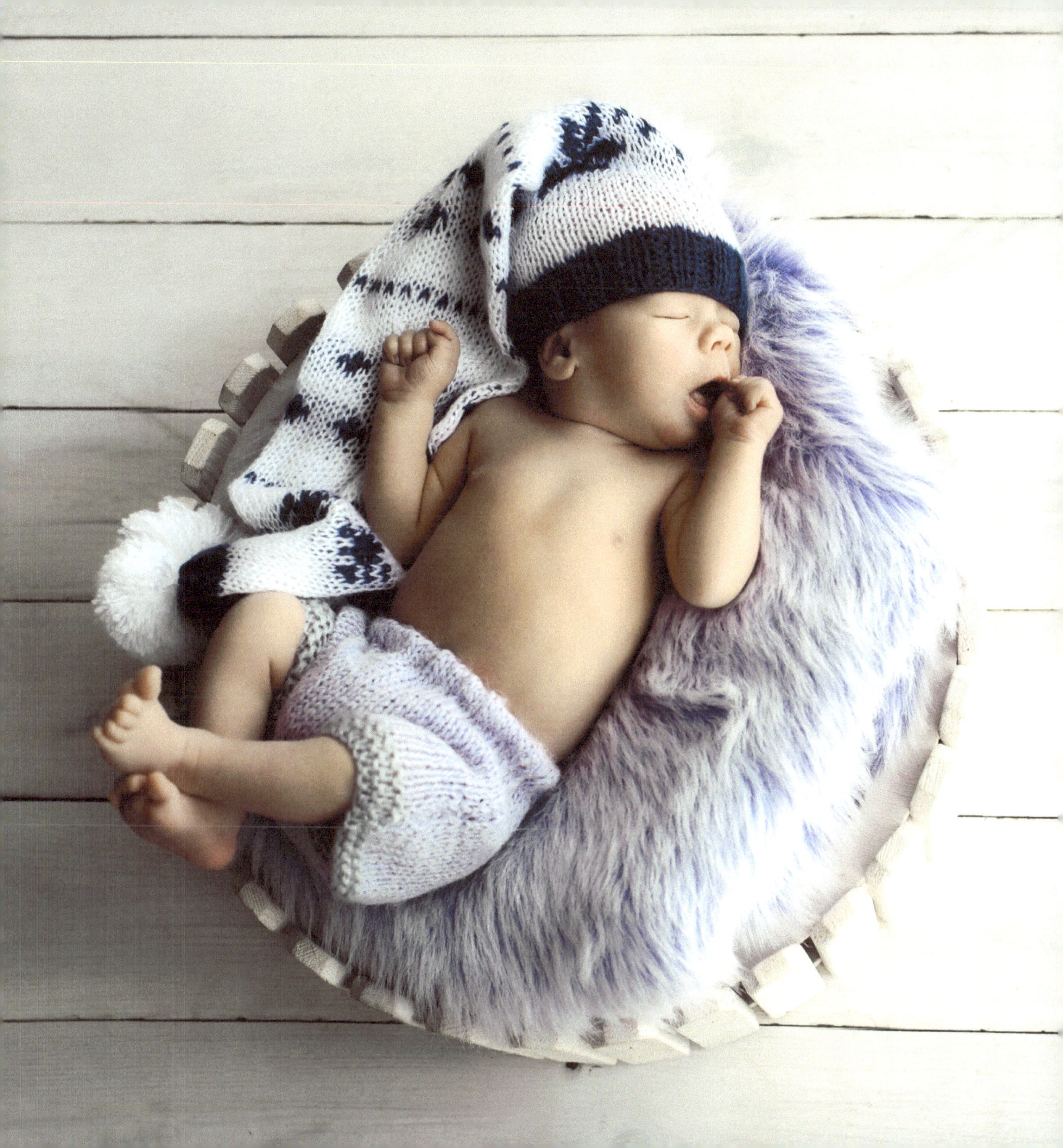

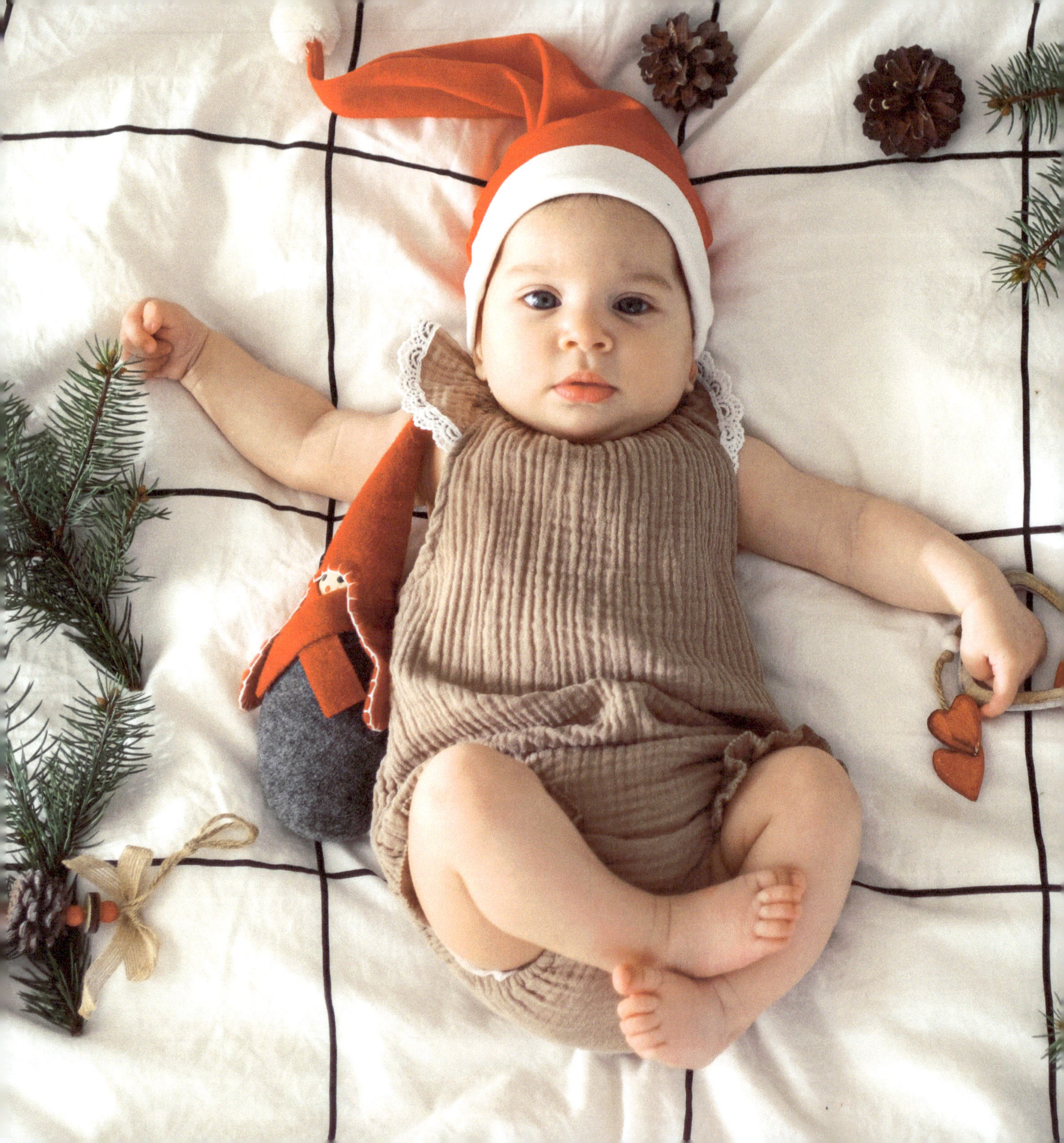

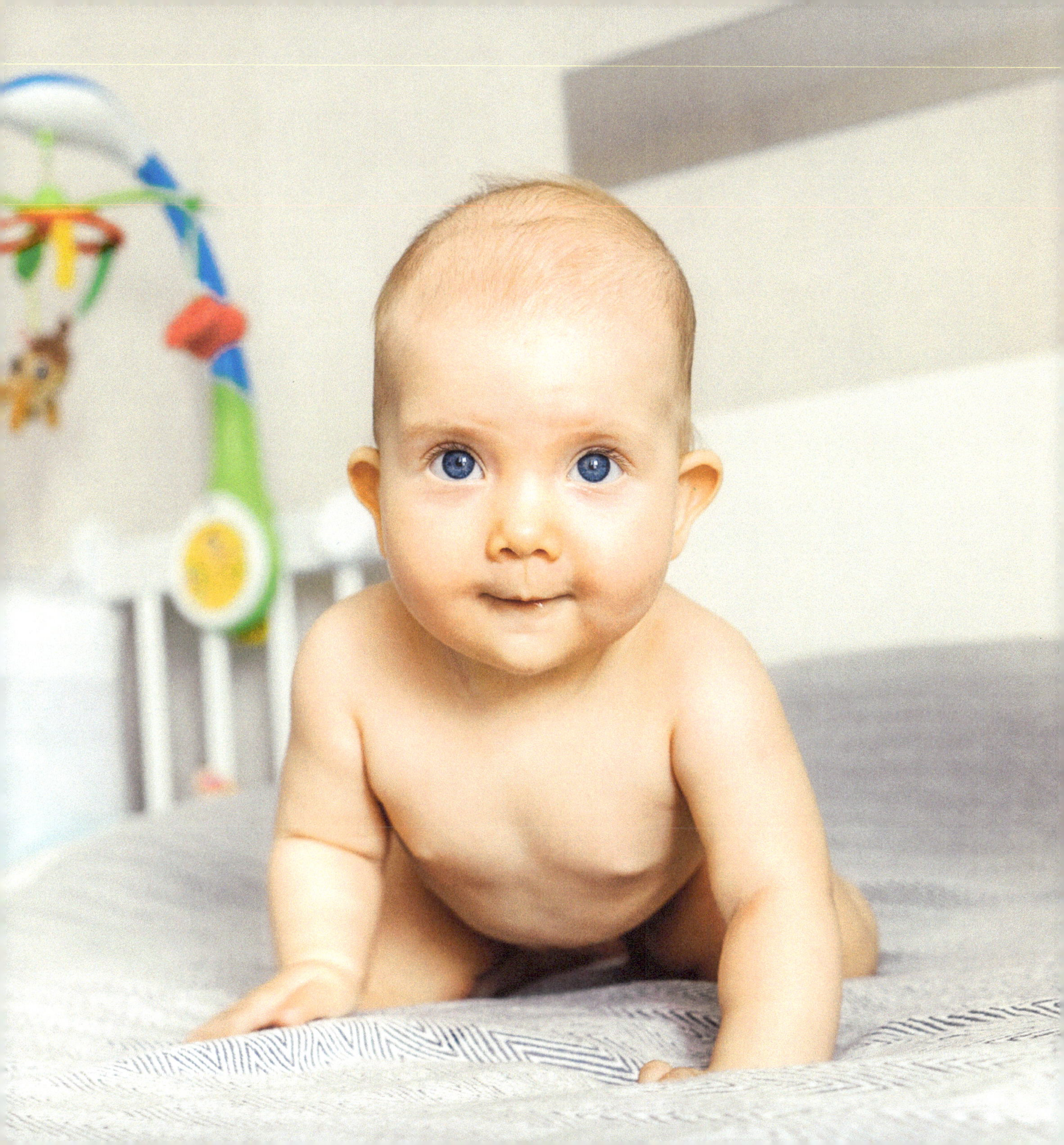

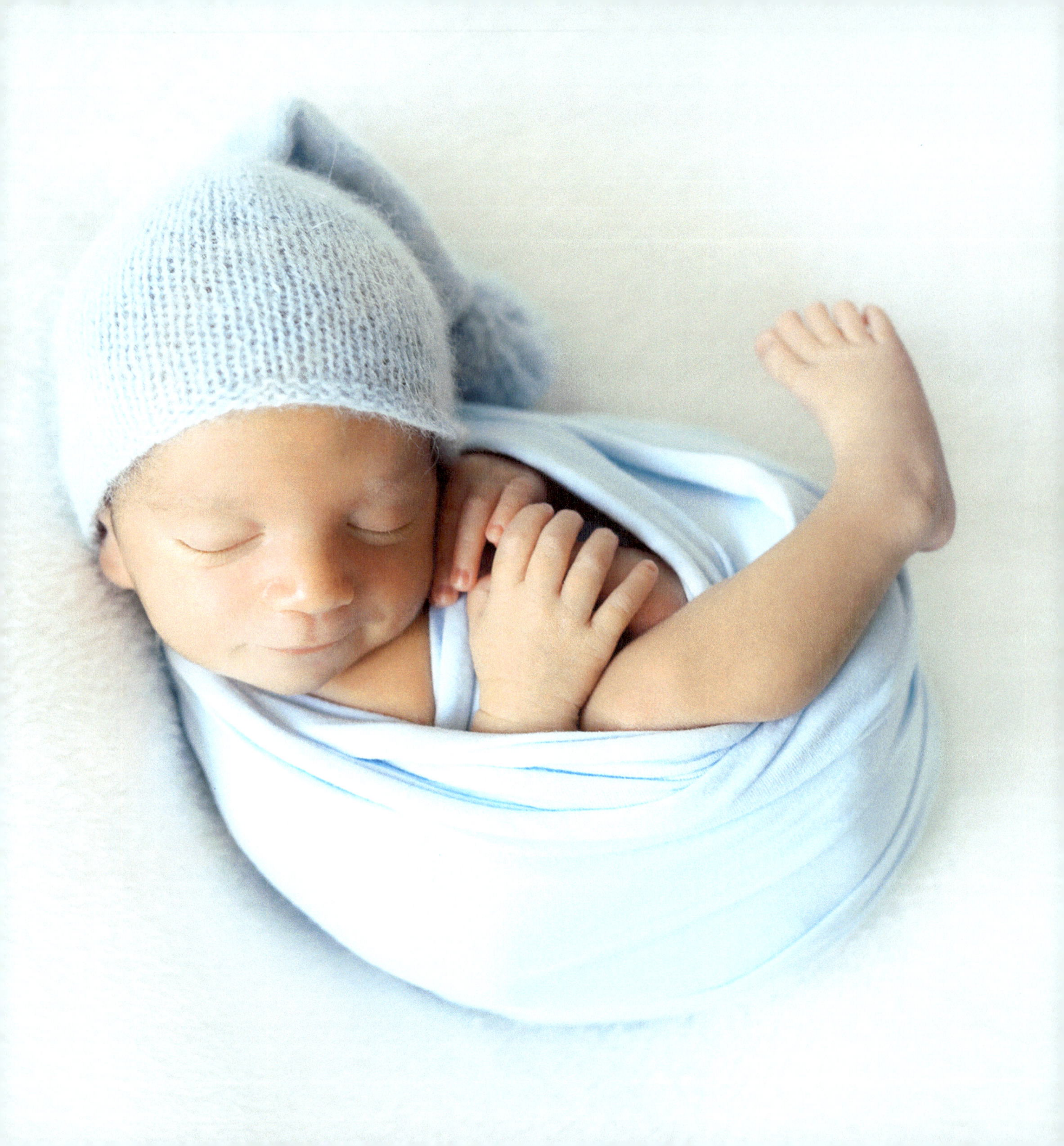

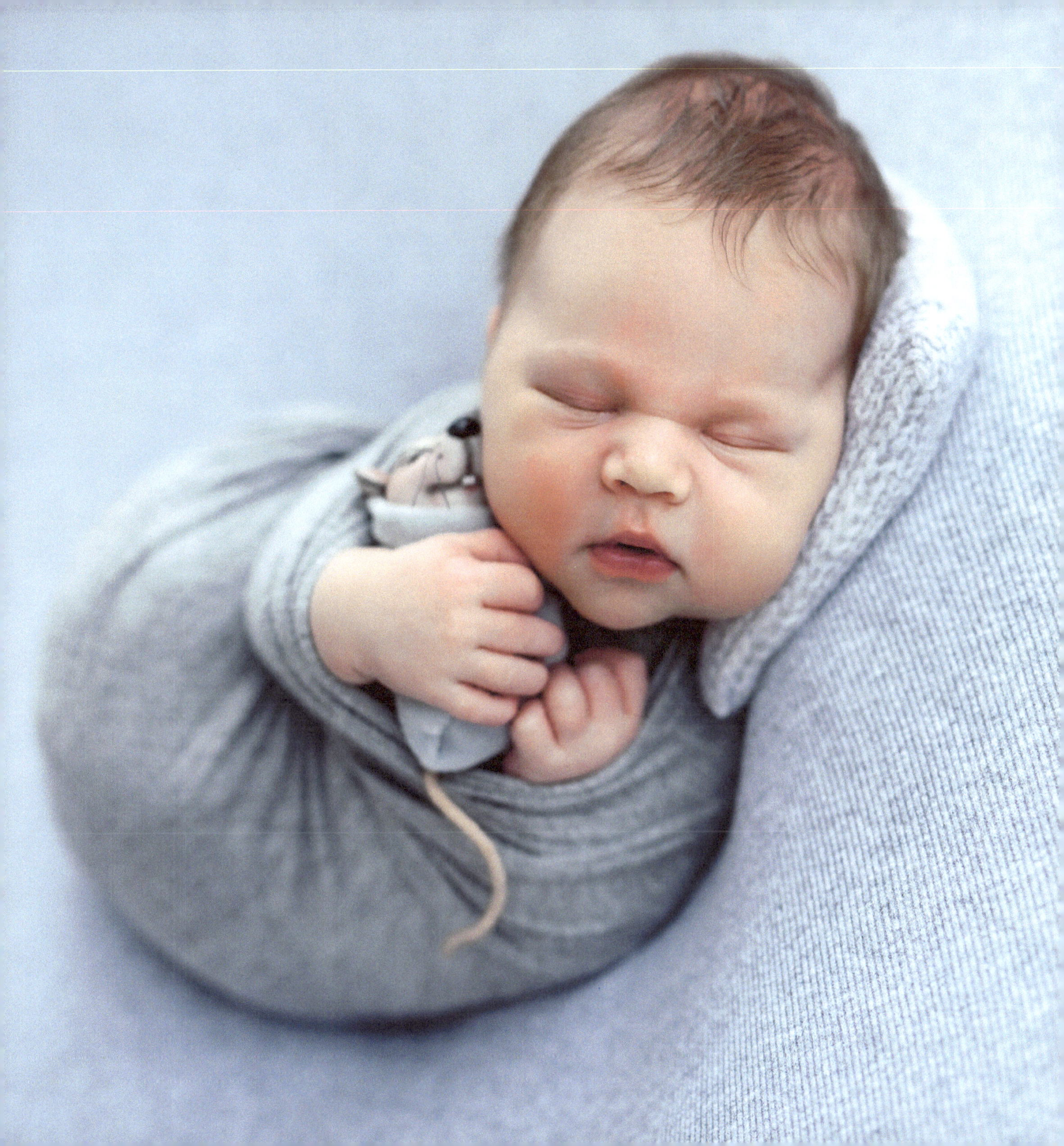

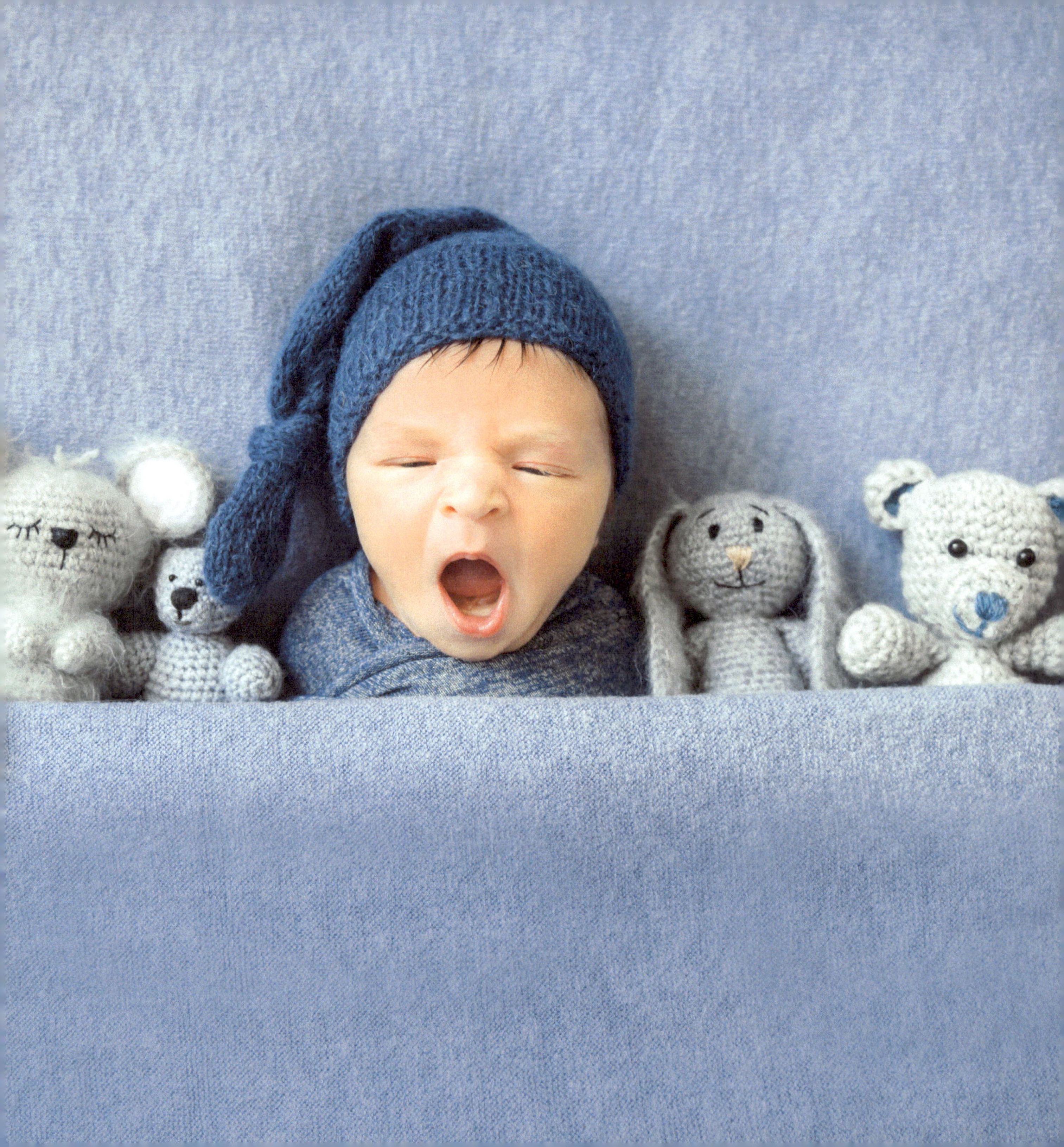

www.ingramcontent.com/pod-product-compliance
Ingram Content Group UK Ltd.
Pitfield, Milton Keynes, MK11 3LW, UK
UKHW061031310726
14089UKWH00009B/192
* 9 7 8 1 9 8 9 8 4 2 1 2 6 *